METROSEXUAL \me-(.)tro - seksh-(e-)wel/ *n*:
1: twenty-first century male trendsetter 2: straight,
urban man with heightened aesthetic sense. 3: man who
spends time and money on appearance and shopping
4: man willing to embrace his feminine side

THE METROSEXUAL
Guide to Style

THE METROSEXUAL
Guide to Style

....

A Handbook for the
Modern Man

....

MICHAEL FLOCKER

DA CAPO PRESS
A Member of the Perseus Books Group

Many of the designations used by manufacturers
and sellers to distinguish their products are
claimed as trademarks. Where those designations appear in this book and Da Capo Press was
aware of a trademark claim, those designations
have been printed with initial capital letters.

Printed in the United States of America.

Text design and illustrations by
George Restrepo and Alex Camlin
Set in 9-point Scotch Roman

Author photograph on
page 170 by Ann Volkwein

Cataloging-in-Publication data for this book is
available from the Library of Congress.

First Edition
ISBN 0-306-81343-2

Published by Da Capo Press
A Member of the Perseus Books Group
http://www.dacapopress.com

Da Capo Press books are available at special dis-
counts for bulk purchases in the U.S. by corpora-
tions, institutions, and other organizations. For
more information, please contact the Special
Markets Department at the Perseus Books
Group, 11 Cambridge Center, Cambridge, MA
02142, or call (800) 255-1514, (617) 252-5298,
or e-mail j.mccrary@perseusbooks.com.

1 2 3 4 5 6 7 8 9–06 05 04 03

We are all in the gutter, but some of us are looking at the stars.

—Oscar Wilde

Contents

I am a major shoe queen.

—Arnold Schwarzenegger, *Vanity Fair*, July 2003

Introduction

Hmm. Interesting. The Terminator has become a shoe queen. What could this possibly mean? Has he tired of crashing through walls and rescuing the masses from the ever-morphing face of evil? Hardly. It is merely a little dash of honesty from a man who knows who he is and who appreciates a good pair of shoes. And whereas it might have been unthinkable ten years ago for a major movie star and an icon of masculinity to amusingly refer to himself as a "queen," it is now simply indicative that Conan is supremely comfortable with himself and deeply in touch with the Zeitgeist.

The once great divide between straight men and gay men has lessened considerably in recent years. As gay men have embraced life at the gym and a more masculine ideal, straight men have begun to realize that they have unnecessarily restricted themselves to the sidelines, clad in a bland uniform of pleated khakis and buttoned-down boredom. It's been slowly realized by both sides that there is a certain power and mystery in ambiguity, and that confidence, security and a sense of style are the defining factors of the modern man. Fear is out and fun is in. Men have come full circle and have met back in the middle at the very point where nature has always intended them to be. After a long and dreary exile, the peacock has reemerged, and things are looking up for all involved.

Throughout history, the very concept of the masculine ideal has been redefined countless times. For centuries pharaohs, kings and czars bedecked themselves in furs and jewels while the underclasses toiled hopelessly clad in dull, flea-bitten rags. The opulent attire and outrageously ornate surroundings of the chosen few were carefully crafted status symbols that unquestionably proclaimed social superiority. But by the dawn of the twentieth century, many of the royal houses of Europe had fallen and the great chasm between the haves and the have-nots had begun to lessen. As the class system began to fade and history continued to steamroll along, the societal roles of both men and women changed accordingly.

During the twentieth century alone, Hollywood trotted out such diverse masculine ideals as Rudolph Valentino, Clark Gable, Cary Grant and Marlon Brando. Each played a pivotal role in defining the masculine ideal of his era. On a more subversive level, popular music also played a part as Elvis, the Beatles and David Bowie all scared the bejesus out of older generations in their respective eras. Men grew their hair, women burned their bras, gays came out of the closet and platform shoes helped raise the profile of the masses. And so it goes.

By the dawn of the twenty-first century, some said that the age of politics and religion was dead, and the age of science and spirituality had arrived. This may or may not have been true, but one thing was certain: The oafish, macho caveman who had been lumbering about the planet looking for a woman to club on the head had been banished to the hinterlands forever. Once again, a new man had emerged and stepped into the spotlight on the ever-shrinking world stage.

The new breed of man is one of style, sophistication and self-awareness. He is just as strong and confident as his predecessor, but far more diverse in his interests, his tastes and most importantly his self-perception. Secure in his masculinity, he no longer has to spend his life defending it. He has options. The sexual revolution is old news and the new man is free to enjoy his single life and his youthful appeal. If he is married, it is by choice, not by necessity, and the walls separating straight men from their gay, fashion-forward brothers are beginning to crumble. More and more, young, urban, straight men are appropriating certain elements of style and culture from the gay community and marketing executives have been quick to catch on. A whole new range of cars, fashions, grooming products, restaurants and sports clubs have been launched to cater to the new man.

As early as the mid-'90s, the writer Mark Simpson coined a new term for this new breed of man—he was the metrosexual. Suddenly, people were writing about him:

Twenty years ago, male fashion, skin care and vanity in general were identified with gay men. Now sexuality, it seems, is irrelevant. In fact, British newspapers have even found a new word for the softer man: the "metrosexual." David Beckham, the man whom British academics have credited with changing male behaviour, has been deemed the ultimate metrosexual. Beckham has helped break "masculine codes," says Warwick University sociology professor Dr. Andrew Parker, "defying various manly expectations such as what clothes a man is allowed to wear."
(Peter Gotting, "The Rise of the Metrosexual," The Age, March 11, 2003)

Though the term may have originated as a seemingly pejorative label, it was quickly adopted as a badge of honor among men who enjoyed their newfound power and heightened visibility. David Beckham, a British soccer superstar, was first identified as the official prototype of the modern metrosexual, yet he was hardly alone in this new world. Famous names such as Brad Pitt, Adrien Brody, Lenny Kravitz, Patrick Rafter, Sean Combs, Ewan MacGregor, Guy Ritchie, Sting, Antonio Banderas, Jason Sehorn and Justin Timberlake all seemed to be clued into the mysterious new rules. In fact, the handlers of most male celebrities were deliberately grooming their clients to fit into this new ideal. Never slaves to fashion or victims of their public image, these men simply understood the power of the images they were projecting and they knew how to play the game.

In today's hip, urban, techno-savvy world, it greatly behooves the average man to get with the program. The degree to which you reinvent yourself is entirely up to you, and while most men will want to stop well short of sarongs and nail polish, a little bit of advice on style, grooming and behavior can't hurt. History has shown that knowledge is the key to success. Whether it is embraced or rejected, knowledge of the game equals power on the playing field, and the men who have shaped the world have always known that.

Long before Wolfgang Amadeus Mozart confounded and aggravated the royal court with his complicated and manic compositions, he was a child prodigy who had mastered the classics of his day. Before Pablo Picasso stood the art world on its misplaced ear, he had studied and painted in the traditional styles. And before Mahatma Gandhi confronted the British establishment clad in little more than a strategically draped cloth, he had received a formal education in England and strode the streets of London in a top hat and cane. By understanding the rules of their respective societies, each of these men was able to rise above those rules, to shatter them and subsequently change the course of history.

To change the course of history, you'll probably require more than the amusing, little handbook you now hold before you. But, regardless of your origin or your chosen path, knowing a little bit about a lot of things is far preferable to staggering blindly through life with goofy shoes and a napkin tucked into your shirt collar. After all, your personal style extends beyond your wardrobe and the contents of your medicine cabinet. Knowledge, social skills, character and a sense of humor are all part of the complete package.

Hopefully the selected wisdoms and insightful nuggets contained herein will raise an eyebrow and add to your already stellar character. After all, no man can know everything, and every man can benefit from a little self-improvement. Just as you regularly upgrade your computer, your car and hopefully your underwear drawer, you can upgrade yourself to become a player in the new era of the modern metrosexual man.

I like to listen.
I have learned a great deal from listening carefully....

...Most people never listen. —Ernest Hemingway

1

General Etiquette

History has shown that even the most accomplished of men have, on occasion, committed well-documented social gaffes. On a visit to England, Jimmy Carter once kissed the Queen Mother on the lips. She was not amused. At a black-tie dinner, Washington Redskin John Riggins urged U.S. Supreme Court Justice Sandra Day O'Connor to "Lighten up, Sandy baby!" That went over like a lead balloon. And in 1992, during a state dinner in Tokyo, George H. W. Bush threw up on the prime minister of Japan. Accidental? Perhaps. But very poor form nonetheless.

Oh No, He Didn't!

It is clear from these cringe-inducing examples that no one is entirely safe from publicly embarrassing oneself. Still it is well worthwhile to master the basics of good etiquette in order to avoid becoming an object of public ridicule. To some, the rules of etiquette may seem outdated, stuffy and unnecessary, but the fact remains that they serve as a sort of social weed-whacker eliminating unsavory growths from popping up in the world's finer gardens. The truth is that first impressions are usually lasting ones, and a bad first impression can sometimes be insurmountable.

In order to live an exciting, varied and culturally diverse life, it behooves the average man to understand and adhere to social customs. Just as a passport opens doors to other countries, good manners and a strong awareness of self can usher you in and out of various social arenas with ease, confidence and comfort. The way that you behave and conduct yourself in social situations is an indicator of your self-awareness and your level of sophistication. And sophistication in its truest sense is not an affectation, but rather an inherent understanding of accepted social behaviors.

Of course, behavioral guidelines are not required in every situation, but it's important to know the rules before you set out to break them. Still, fate can be cruel at the strangest times, and unforeseen fiascos may put your dignity to the test, but if you're going to fall down the stairs, you might as well do so with a little style and a dash of panache.

Formal Functions

Most social occasions, regardless of their formality, are meant to be entertaining and fun. Feeling edgy, nervous or hesitant at such functions is usually the result of uncertainty. What do

I say? How should I dress? What do I do with this olive pit? Social perils such as these are easily dealt with if you behave in a calm and logical manner. It isn't rocket science and you don't need a degree from Oxford to enjoy yourself at the party.

Possibly the most important factor in determining your comfort level is knowing that you are appropriately dressed for the occasion. As a general rule, you will always feel a bit better being slightly overdressed than underdressed. Invitations to formal affairs will usually include an indication of the dress code. If none is indicated, you know you've got some leeway, but it never hurts to ask others if you're uncertain. Just remember that if you feel confident in how you look, that's one less thing to worry about. If you're simply clueless, go for black.

At the most formal of occasions, when being introduced to others or making introductions, it is customary to introduce on the basis of one's social status. This means the guest is presented to the bride, the associate to the boss, and the movie star to the queen. Socially speaking, the man should be presented to the woman, and the significantly younger person should be introduced to the older. Always remember, an introduction is meant to open the lines of communication, it is not a call to launch into a monologue. A simple "How do you do" is usually a sensible start.

Once you're in the door and on the scene, your job as a guest is to be self-sufficient, make friends and add to the occasion. You don't want to stand around sulking and waiting to be trotted around. You should be open to meeting and mingling, friendly and outgoing. Even if it's not your scene, make an effort and you'll find someone to talk to. If for any reason you feel intimidated or unsure, just smile and be a good listener. Playing shy can sometimes be a good buffer and, if done well, can even be quite endearing.

The best advice is just to relax and observe. Don't panic if you find yourself standing alone—you can always stroll around, check out the view or admire the paintings, while maintaining your confident and approachable demeanor. Good mingling means floating around and keeping things light. Just keep your cool and remember the basic rules of conduct:

- It is always better to be slightly overdressed than underdressed.
- Arriving late is rude, but so is arriving early; 15–20 minutes after the stated start time is ideal for social occasions.
- Be polite, and don't assume too much familiarity with other guests too soon.
- Be a self-sufficient guest, and take advantage of the opportunity to meet new people.
- If the conversation is over your head, shut up, listen and smile.
- Always be kind and friendly to the staff.
- Do not tag along with other guests unless invited to do so.
- Do not molest the other guests.
- Be sure to leave before the lights come up.
- Always thank the host and say goodnight to those you've met.
- If you're blotto, get out of there pronto with as few witnesses as possible.
- (Oh, and as for that olive pit, wrap it in your cocktail napkin and hold onto it until you find an appropriate place to discreetly dispose of it.)

Table Manners

Okay, so you may never get invited to Buckingham Palace, but chances are you will attend a few dinner parties, weddings or other social dining affairs in your lifetime. While good manners rarely draw attention, bad manners can be spotted at a hundred yards and send a honking signal that you are out of your element. Even at the most casual affairs, if you know proper form, you can relax and loosen up at will, knowing that it's a conscious choice on your part.

To avoid embarrassing yourself, it is wise to remember a few very simple rules and guidelines that can be easily and casually incorporated into your behavior. No grand flourishes or pinched facial expressions are necessary. Just be careful, be quiet and always remember:

- Make sure your cell phone is turned off, and your attention is focused on the other guests.
- Wait for the host to indicate where you may be seated, or at least follow the lead of others.
- Once seated, place your napkin on your lap. If you leave the table, place it on your chair.
- Wait for the host to pick up their fork before eating, unless urged to do otherwise.
- Pass to the right and never reach across the table.
- With silverware, work your way in. The outside fork is for salad, the next one in is for the entrée, etc.
- Do not blow on or slurp soup. Spoon the soup away from yourself, and tip the bowl away from your body for the final spoonful.
- When eating meat, poultry or fish, slice a piece or two at a time and take a bite. Do not slice it all up at once.
- Try to keep pace with everyone else. You don't want to inhale your food and be the first one done, or talk so much that you're the last one eating.
- Never speak with your mouth full, no matter how excited you are to join the conversation.

Cell Phone Etiquette

- When in the company of others, keep calls to an absolute minimum.
- Always turn your phone off in restaurants, cinemas and museums.
- If you need to make a call, excuse yourself and step outside.
- Keep your voice down in public. Don't shout out your business for all to hear.

- Used silverware should never be placed back on the tablecloth. When finished, place your utensils together pointed in the direction of 11:00.

- Forearms on the edge of the table are acceptable at formal affairs, and the old rule about elbows on the table is pretty much a thing of the past, especially in casual situations. Even so, be aware of the actions of those around you and act accordingly.

Cocktail Parties

In most cases, cocktail parties are fairly casual affairs, though a stuffy crowd or a pristine setting can certainly drag down the fun quotient. But in such scenarios, the fun lies in observation and investigation. Enjoy the show and chances are you'll find someone to have a good giggle with.

Whether in someone's home, at an art gallery, in a business setting or a royal palace, common sense should serve you well. The thing to remember is that there are ears and eyes everywhere, so you should avoid gossiping too loudly or laughing at the paintings because you never know who's standing behind you.

As for mingling, you should feel free to flirt and chat with anyone you'd like to meet, but you need to be subtle in your approach. The clumsiest thing you can do is to interrupt a conversation. It's best to wait for an opening and have something in mind to say when it's time to dive in. Opening with a question or a compliment is usually a safe bet.

In a business setting, it is perfectly appropriate to exchange business cards at the end of the evening if the conversation justifies it. Networking and making contacts is often part of the game, and while you can never fully disguise the fact that you have some goal in mind, it is rarely a good idea to make requests or ask for a favor in a social setting. That's what the card is for. It says, "I'd like to talk business with you at some other time." Then again, sometimes it means, "Call me some-time and we can get nasty."

When you're out in public, caution is always the key word. Some other things to keep in mind at a cocktail party:

- If hors d'oeuvres are served, always take a napkin and carry it with you. Do the same with cocktails.
- Try not to respond to questions with just a yes or no. The idea is to keep the ball rolling.
- Be upbeat, outgoing and friendly, but try not to get overly excited or dominate the conversation.
- Always be subtle and discreet when flirting. It will help preserve your dignity if the interest is not returned. Be yourself. Clenched jaws, fake accents and grand gestures can only lead to humiliation and social ruin.
- Try to avoid in-depth discussions of politics, religion and money. If these subjects do come up, keep things light and steer clear of serious debate.
- Don't reveal too much about yourself. No one wants to hear about your recent tragic breakup, your awkward medical maladies or your ghastly family.
- If you get trapped in a conversation, just excuse yourself to go to the bathroom or to greet another guest.
- Don't make an ass of yourself just because the drinks are free. Pace yourself and watch out for low-hanging mobiles and ceiling fans.
- Don't dance if you don't know how.

The European Air Kiss

You've seen it on television countless times at the Oscars, on talk shows and even in political situations, and though it may seem to be an affectation, it is a common greeting in various social settings and international cultures, and it shouldn't throw you for a loop. A quick review of proper form should help you avoid butting heads or mistaking an innocent greeting as a come-on.

The air kiss usually begins with a joining of hands and then a quick peck on *both* cheeks. Sometimes it's just one cheek, but you should be prepared for a double. You don't want to walk away just as the other person is leaning in for a two-cheeker and send them staggering off into a potted plant.

Another thing to remember is that the peck is not really a peck so much as a touching of the cheek. Under no circumstances should you plant a big, fat, wet one on a stranger. A light touch is important so that you don't mar a woman's makeup or send the wrong signal to a man, and in certain social settings or cultures you may end up greeting other men this way, so don't panic. It doesn't mean anything, just keep it dry.

The Perfect Gentleman

In social settings as well as business settings, behaving like a gentleman will serve you well and will give others the impression that you are a person of good breeding who is confident and self-assured. Even if this is a false impression, it's a good one, and it will surely benefit you whether the situation is romantic or professional. Following a simple code of ten behaviors will keep you on track and prevent you from appearing boorish or crass:

Always be punctual. While social occasions offer more leeway, punctuality is essential for business situations. Better to be a bit early and walk around the block or stop by the men's room to check on your appearance.

Shake hands firmly. This does not mean crushing the other person's hand, or shaking it with such vigor that their head wobbles. Just connect solidly, smile and look the person in the eye.

Be polite at all times. Saying "Excuse me," "Please" and "Thank you" should be second nature, and you should always be courteous even when others are being irritating or rude. Always take the high road and you'll come out on top.

Do not interrupt. In conversation, it is rude to interrupt or speak over others. If you do so inadvertently, you should simply excuse yourself, and listen carefully until it is your turn to speak.

Do not swear in public. Though you may enjoy talking trash with your friends, you should never use foul language in a business encounter or at a formal affair. Always keep in mind that swearing repeatedly gives the impression that you have a very limited vocabulary.

Never raise your voice. You should be aware of your vocal volume at all times when in public. Not only because it is rude to speak loudly, but you also don't want everyone in the room to hear your conversation.

Always control your temper. In any situation, it is extremely unseemly to argue or lose your cool in front of others. No one should be subjected to your temper tantrums, and you never want to give the impression that you are an emotional basket case who can't control himself. If a situation arises, let the other guy lose control.

Never discuss or display money. Your income and the amount of cash in your wallet are both private matters. You should not discuss your wealth (or lack thereof), nor should you wave around wads of bills.

Never groom yourself in public. If you need to blow your nose, have something stuck in your teeth or need to rearrange some part of your person, always excuse yourself and tend to the matter in the privacy of the nearest bathroom.

Always tip well and say thank you for service. Not only will it be appreciated, it will also ensure good service the next time around. That said, do so discreetly without drawing attention to yourself.

Tipping

In most service industries, tipping is a gesture of appreciation that constitutes a large portion of the server's income. And given the fact that these people will be handling your food, altering your appearance or ensuring the safekeeping of your luggage, it pays to tip appropriately. As a rule, there are no circumstances where a tip should be less than a dollar. To leave change behind is as rude as leaving nothing at all.

In those rare situations when it is unclear whether tipping is customary, you should guess in the 15 to 20 percent range. If tipping is inappropriate in a given situation, chances are a horrified expression will be your first clue. If so, that's fine. Now you know. As for standard tipping, here's a general breakdown:

Restaurant Maitre d' It is not necessary to tip just for being seated, but if you have asked for favors or received exceptional treatment, tipping is optional. If you do decide to tip, discretion is absolutely essential to avoid embarrassing everyone involved. And *never* offer a tip to the owner of the restaurant.

Waiter At least 15 to 20 percent of the total bill including tax. More for exceptional service.

Bartender 1 to 2 dollars per drink depending on the setting and price of the drinks. For tabs, 15 to 20 percent, and on free rounds you should leave roughly half the value of the round.

Cocktail Server Usually 1 to 2 dollars per drink depending on setting.

Valet Parking 2 to 5 dollars on top of the parking fee.

Taxi/Shuttle Drivers 10 to 20 percent of the fare.

Limousine Driver 15 to 20 percent of total bill.

Airport Skycap 1 to 2 dollars per bag.

Hotel Bellman 1 to 3 dollars per bag, depending upon the hotel.

Hotel Room Service 15 to 20 percent (check the bill to see if the gratuity is included).

Hotel Maid 1 to 10 dollars per night depending on the hotel and your personal habits (in an envelope if one is provided or left on the pillow).

Hairstylist 15 to 20 percent.

Shampoo Assistant 2 to 3 dollars.

Masseur/Masseuse 10 to 20 percent.

Casino Dealer A 5 dollar chip per gambling session (more at high-stakes tables, and a lot more if you win big).

Travel Etiquette

One of the greatest things you can do in life for sheer pleasure as well as education is to travel abroad. And though you might assume that international travel is highly expensive, the clever metrosexual knows that it is often comparable in price to traveling to another American city. To experience other cultures and to understand what it is to be the foreigner can be a revelation. On the other hand, traveling within a country as large as the United States can be an eye-opener, too. Visiting new cities can often seem like traveling to another country, and there is always plenty to see.

While tropical getaways and retreats to wide-open spaces are essential from time to time, the metrosexual man, by definition, has a particular affinity for the excitement and diversity of the world's great metropolitan centers. Where restaurants, nightlife, shopping, culture, architecture and history are concerned, there are certain international hubs that are in a class of their own and should be on every metro-man's lifetime must-see list.

Top Ten Metrosexual Destinations

New York Because it is unlike any other city. The excitement and energy are legendary and the variety of restaurants, museums, nightclubs and shopping opportunities is unparalleled.

London Because it's swinging again. History collides with high style in the sprawling metropolis renowned for its unique charm, scandalous tabloids and great music.

Paris Because it's Paris. Beautiful people, high fashion, amazing museums and some of the most beautiful architecture in the world keep this city at the top of the list.

Barcelona Because it has emerged as one of the most beautiful and cosmopolitan cities in Europe. The laid-back Mediterranean pace, spectacular architecture, buzzing nightlife and fabulous weather seal the deal.

Los Angeles Because it's show biz, babe. Beautiful people, big money, power lunches, swimming pools and movie stars keep the dream alive in Tinseltown.

Miami Because the city reinvented itself. Pastel colors, Deco-decadence mixed with '50s chic, world-class hotels and an international social scene put South Beach back on the map.

Milan Because it's the fashion capital of Italy. That means a sea of supermodels, café culture, nightlife, dining and out-of-this-world shopping. Don't come back without a new pair of shoes.

San Francisco Because of its bohemian history. The compact metropolis is one-of-a-kind with its colorful neighborhoods, fantastic restaurants, coffeehouse culture, underground energy and spectacular natural beauty.

Amsterdam Because decadence is fun. The ultra-liberal ways of the Dutch make this charming city of winding canals, "coffeehouses," bicycles, sex shops and nightclubs a unique experience. World-class art museums and fascinating architecture provide the balance.

Marrakech Because there is life beyond Europe and the U.S. When it's time to slow down, dry out and unwind, Morocco's exotic culture, ancient history, ornate palaces and unhurried pace provide the perfect setting.

International Travel

Though the full tour of international hot spots may be beyond your reach, you'll still want to see as much as you can. To see the world is to develop an international awareness that your life has infinite possibilities. There is a global community out there and you want to be a part of it to whatever degree possible. But to travel to another culture and expect the customs and behaviors of the locals to be like those at home is simply naïve.

There is a commonly held misconception that Parisians are always very rude to Americans visiting their city. This notion has been perpetuated over the years, but is not always the case. Parisians can be as kind, helpful and friendly as the residents of any other major city. It is true, however, that they can be very rude to American tourists who are rude to them.

The truth is that whether in France or any other part of the world, the manner in which you conduct yourself plays a huge part in how you are received. There is one simple rule when traveling abroad that you must always keep in mind: *You are the guest.* Act like one, and things will go much more smoothly.

Do your best to communicate with the locals and be as courteous as possible.

Don't treat them like aliens who don't speak English. You are the alien, and chances are they can understand what you are saying.

Travel Dos and Don'ts

Do be respectful of the local culture and be patient with service.
Don't become demanding and paranoid that you are being mistreated.

Do make an effort to appreciate and experiment with the local cuisine.
Don't insist on American condiments or make complicated requests.

Do dress like an adult, try to blend in and represent your country with dignity.
Don't go to a museum or restaurant in a tank top and gym shorts.

Do protect your valuables and be aware of safety.
Don't draw attention to yourself with goofy fanny packs or money belts stuffed into your underpants.

Do your best to communicate with locals and be as courteous as possible.
Don't treat them like aliens who don't speak English. You are the alien, and chances are they can understand what you're saying.

Trekking on a Budget

In an ideal world, you might envision yourself flying first-class, staying in four-star hotels, frequenting only the most exclusive restaurants and nightclubs, and returning home with an extra suitcase filled with your expensive holiday purchases. But the truth is that a trip like that is not the only way to go. The seasoned traveler knows that such luxuries are entirely unnecessary to having a grand old time.

By making a few compromises and planning intelligently, you can see it all without breaking the bank. The most important thing is to get there and enjoy whatever is available to you. If you're traveling on a budget, keep the following tips in mind:

THE METROSEXUAL GUIDE TO STYLE

- Find a decent one- or two-star hotel located in a good area. You're going to be out and about every day, so you really just need a place to sleep.
- Invest in a Eurail pass when visiting Europe. You can get unlimited travel for a limited time for a few hundred dollars. It's the cheapest way to see several countries in one trip.
- Save money by eating lunch on the fly, and save your cash for a couple of nice dinners out.
- Spend your days doing the free stuff. Explore the city, visit museums and historic sites, find street fairs, festivals and markets. You'll have more to spend on nightlife.
- Keep a bottle of wine and some snacks in your hotel room to cut back on expenses.
- Go shopping without buying. Then at the end of your stay, go back and buy the one or two items you want the most.
- Walk everywhere.

When in Rome . . .

As a guest in a foreign land, it is your obligation to learn at least a few words in the local language. This doesn't take much effort—most travel books have a glossary of helpful phrases that if humbly attempted will at least indicate an effort on your part. As often as not, your mangling of the language will result in a quick rescue as the bemused bartender or vendor offers to help you out in broken English. The key is not to storm in and bellow, "Do you speak English?" If you have to ask, try to do so in the local tongue.

13
phrases to know
in any
foreign language
....

Yes

No

Excuse me

Please

Thank you

Do you speak English?

I would like . . .
(then you can point)

How much?

Where is the . . . ?

What's your name?

You're very sexy

My hotel is nearby

Get out

General Etiquette: The Bottom Line

Being a guest, whether in someone's home or in a foreign land, means behaving respectfully and with appreciation. By assuming a reasonable level of humility, as opposed to arrogant entitlement, you are far more likely to find yourself received in a friendly and hospitable manner.

When I read about the evils of drinking,....

...*I gave up reading.* —Henny Youngman

2

Wine & Cocktails

At the various dinners, cocktail parties and social soirees he attends, the metrosexual man is often surrounded by a kaleidoscopic array of wines and cocktails from which to choose. What he drinks, if in fact he chooses to drink, can be as telling as the watch on his wrist or the shoes on his feet. Assuming that keg parties and beer busts are securely tucked away in your past, a little review of the basics may be in order. After all, an informed selection is always preferable to a bad guess when buying a bottle of wine as a gift or ordering cocktails at the latest hot spot.

Wine 101

Like many things in life, an appreciation of wine is an acquired sensibility. Many who have once stated that they don't care for wine often find their minds changed when they are introduced to finer vintages. If you intend to broaden your horizons in any aspect of life, you need to be open to experimentation and take advantage of opportunities to try new things. You may be in for some very pleasant surprises.

One of the most treacherous stumbling blocks for the novice sophisticate is the much-dreaded wine list. Though there is an entire universe of fine wines to explore, knowing the basics should help prevent blank stares and helpless shrugs. Whether in a restaurant or a wine shop, the key is to have one or two choices in mind going in.

The Three Basic Categories

Table Wines The general term for the most commonly consumed wines. These are the reds and the whites that are usually served with a meal. Generally speaking, whites are served chilled, and reds are served at room temperature. Reds are aged, but whites are generally not.

Sparkling Wines These are the "bubbly" wines usually served on special occasions. Champagne is made exclusively from grapes grown in the Champagne region of France. "Sparkling" wines are made throughout the world using the same techniques as those used in the creation of champagne, but with different grapes.

Fortified Wines Created by adding wine alcohol or brandy, fortified wines such as port and sherry are heavier, and usually served with desserts or as an after-dinner drink.

The Most Common Whites

White wines are generally perceived to be lighter and airier than reds, and so are popular choices in summer months when the temperature is rising. However, the white/red rules are flexible, and it is the combination of meal and wine that should dictate your choice. Lighter fare is generally complemented by white wines.

Chardonnay Perhaps the most popular of the whites, chardonnays are so-named after a variety of grape. Most often a full-bodied, fruity wine that may have hints of oak, butter and green apple, chardonnays are usually fermented and briefly aged in oak barrels.

Best bet when buying: California label

Chablis A general term for a light, white table wine from the Chablis region in northern France. Many Chablis are made from Chardonnay grapes, and the term itself is more frequently used in Britain than the United States.

Best bet when buying: French label

Pinot Grigio (or Pinot Gris) Named after a variety of white grape, a Pinot Grigio is a light, tangy, dry white often with hints of apple or pear. At times it may also have touches of citrus or even light spice, and has a light and refreshing character.

Best bet when buying: Italian label

Riesling A light white, often lower in alcohol, Rieslings are relatively sweet and have a light, floral aroma. With occasional hints of peach or melon, most originate in Germany though they are also made in France and Austria.

Best bet when buying: German label

Sauvignon Blanc A fairly light, dry white with hints of lemongrass, green herbs or even grapefruit that is considered to be the opposite of Chardonnay. California vintners sometimes use the term *fume blanc* to describe their version of a Sauvignon Blanc.

Best bet when buying: French label

ᴊМᴏꜱᴛ Cᴏᴍᴍᴏɴ ᴿᴇᴅꜱ

Code Red—
A Word of Warning
After drinking several glasses of red wine, check yourself in the bathroom mirror as a thin black line may have mysteriously appeared on your lower lip. It's not a discovery you want to make at home after the evening is over.

Red wines are heartier than whites, and are therefore a very cozy choice during a winter snowstorm. However, there's nothing wrong with ordering a nice red in the warm glow of summer if the mood strikes you.

Cabernet Named after the classic red grape variety, the very popular cabernet is a smooth, hearty red that may exhibit hints of black currant, oak or black cherry. Made throughout the world, some cabernets also have hints of cedar wood and plum.

Best bet when buying: California label

Chianti A crisp, dry, Italian red wine named after the Chianti region in Tuscany. Once identified with the basket-bottle and red, checkered tablecloths, Chiantis sold in the U.S. have grown more sophisticated, and are an excellent choice for those seeking a slightly tart, but light and tangy red.

Best bet when buying: Italian label

Merlot The Merlot grape is similar to the cabernet grape, though slightly softer and plumper. The wine is rich, aromatic and full-bodied with hints of rose, oak, plum and even chocolate. Merlots are frequently blended with Cabernet Sauvignons.

Best bet when buying: California label

Pinot Noir Considered lighter than merlot and cabernet, the pinot noir variety of grape yields a light, fruity wine with suggestions of berries, violets and very light spice. Made in various countries, it is characterized by earthy aromas and a silky texture.

Best bet when buying: French, Washington or Oregon label

Zinfandel A red grape used in the creation of mild-tasting wines that range in color from light pink to bright red. Sweet and fruity, with strong berry hints and light spice, zinfandels are not usually the first choice of the connoisseur, though high-end labels are gaining in prestige.

Best bet when buying: California or Australian label

Ordering Wines in Restaurants

When faced with the crucial choice of ordering a nice bottle of wine to go with your romantic evening out, you needn't panic. If you're worried about making the wrong selection for your meal, you always have the option of asking your date what they're interested in ordering and then asking the waiter what he'd recommend with such a meal. If you'd rather choose yourself, simply follow the most commonly accepted rules of thumb at right.

How to Order

When ordering wine in a restaurant, you will usually have a choice between ordering by the glass, in a carafe or by the bottle. When ordering by the glass, you always have the option of ordering the house red or white. This is the restaurant's standard choice, and it is usually a reasonably priced chardonnay or cabernet. It's a safe bet if you're not in the mood to splurge.

Carafes are usually offered in two sizes: a half-liter, which will fill about three glasses, and a liter, which will fill about six. Always a good option if you want more than a glass or two, but less than a full bottle, or when ordering for large groups sharing wine.

**White wines
go best with**

....

Chicken

Fish

Salads

Pastas served in cream sauces

Japanese or Thai cuisine

**Red wines
go best with**

....

Red meats

Cheeses and pâtés

Stews

Pastas in tomato sauces

Pheasant or other game birds

When ordering a bottle, there is the usual ritual of presentation and tasting. This is the point in the evening where one false move can result in a most unpleasant eyeball rolling by the waiter. There are a few tips to keep in mind that will help you avoid being exposed:

Look at the label and nod.

Don't sniff.

- If a strange man or woman appears bearing a wine list, chances are you may have encountered the sommelier. In high-end establishments, it is this person's job to help you with your wine selection. Smile, listen and then make your own decision.
- The waiter will hold the bottle before you for your approval. Remain calm—this is not some sort of quiz. Just glance at the label and nod that he has brought the correct bottle.
- He will uncork the wine and place the cork on the table. Do not pick it up and sniff it. If he offers it to you, just take a look. A rotted cork is a sign that the wine has been "corked" and should not be drunk.
- He will pour a sampling in your glass. Do not hold it up to the light. You don't know what you're looking for, so don't pretend. You may try a sip and nod your approval, but it is also acceptable to just smell the wine and place the glass back on the table. If the wine is off or simply unacceptable, this is the time to send it back. Otherwise, just smile and nod knowingly, and he will fill the glasses.
- An attentive waiter will keep an eye on the table and stop by to refill glasses, but it's perfectly all right for you to keep the good times flowing. If you do pour the wine yourself, never fill the glass to the top. A regular wine glass should never be more than three-quarters full, and large "balloon" glasses for reds should only be filled a third of the way.

When it comes to drinking wines, go slowly. They are to be sipped, savored and appreciated, not guzzled as a thirst quencher. If you're thirsty, just ask the waiter for some water to go along with the wine.

Choosing Wisely at the Wine Shop

When selecting wine as a gift, there is a blissfully simple rule that also applies to shoes and automobiles. You tend to get what you pay for. This is not to imply that you need to spend a great deal of money to impress. On the contrary, there are very good wines out there for fifteen dollars or less, so there's no reason to go overboard. But always remember that what's on sale is usually that which is not selling very well.

Decide in advance what you would like to buy based on the occasion. Then approach any member of the staff and ask for help. There is no reason to feel intimidated or embarrassed. Most likely they will be happy to help, offer a great suggestion and you may learn something. Better to have the wine shop employee know you're clueless, rather than the party guests.

If you're on a date, chances are that you and your intended will open the wine and have a nice time. If you are attending a party, just give the bottle to your host and join in the fun. Don't stand around waiting for your bottle to be opened so that you can be praised and applauded. It's a gift, and they may open it or save it for another occasion.

Cocktail Universe

Personal preference in regard to cocktails is something you will have to explore over time. With the infinite variety of liquors and mixers available, there are countless cocktails from which to choose. The best advice is to keep it simple, lest you end up standing against the wall with an embarrassing concoction adorned with umbrellas and plastic monkeys.

Most restaurants and bars offer many liquors. The various brands are usually divided into three categories: well, call and top shelf. If you order a vodka and tonic, you will receive the standard-grade, house vodka. That is the well brand. If you want something better, you must specify and order by name brand—an "Absolut and tonic" or a "Stoli on the rocks." Top shelf simply refers to the best brand on offer, so you may ask the bartender, "What is your top-shelf Scotch?"

Martinis

There are some cocktails that have a certain James Bond quality and are classics of the cocktail universe. Chief among these is the martini, which is a simple cocktail made of vodka or gin and dry vermouth, served with an olive or a lemon rind. It is the amount of vermouth that determines how "dry" the martini is—the less vermouth, the drier the drink.

When ordering martinis there are always distinctions. If you simply order a martini, chances are you'll get vodka, so if you want gin, order a gin martini. Martinis usually come with an olive. If you want the lemon rind you should specify "with a twist." A "dirty" martini comes with one or more olives and a splash of olive juice to dirty it up. A martini with an onion is a gimlet, and a martini with no vermouth, a splash of cranberry and lime juice is a cosmopolitan.

There are also apple martinis, chocolate martinis and many other variations made by adding liqueurs to the mix, though a clear-thinking metrosexual will always choose dirty over fruity. Confusing, perhaps, but whatever you do, don't say "Shaken, not stirred." Nobody stirs martinis anymore and the bartender will hate you.

Whiskeys and Bourbons

The differences between whiskey, scotch and bourbon are a bit tricky. While all bourbons are whiskeys, not all whiskeys are bourbons. The origins of the whiskeys, the combination of grains, the processing and the age of the blend are the factors that distinguish one from the other:

- Canadian whiskeys are lighter in taste and color, and are aged at least four years before export. Popular brands include Canadian Club and Black Velvet. Irish whiskeys, such as Bushmills and Jameson, are a slightly heavier blend.
- Scotch is a blended whiskey with a slightly smokey flavor. Aged for at least four years before export, scotch is made exclusively in Scotland and popular brands include Dewars and Johnnie Walker. Single malt scotches, such as Glenlivet and Glenfiddich, are often the choice of true connoisseurs. The longer single malts are aged, the better they are presumed to be.
- Bourbon is a sweeter and heavier whiskey that derives its name from Bourbon County, Kentucky, where it originated. Popular brands include Jim Beam and Maker's Mark.

Gins and Vodkas

The two most popular "light liquors" are usually served with mixers on the rocks. In the home, vodka (and gin if you so choose) should be stored in the freezer. The level of alcohol will prevent it from freezing, and it will preserve it at the perfect temperature for cocktails. It is believed by many that gin and vodka are less likely to cause hangovers than dark liquors because of their lower sugar content and charcoal filtration processes. Only time and trial can prove whether this is true for you.

- Gin is a distilled liquor flavored with juniper that first became fashionable as a cocktail in seventeenth-century England. Different brands are distinguished by various mixes of botanicals, including spices, herbs and fruits. While some creative bartenders have incorporated it into cocktails, the standard gin and tonic is the true classic with Tanqueray and Bombay among the most popular brands.

- Vodka derives its name from the Russian *voda* ("water of life"), and its existence has been documented as far back as the ninth century. Today many brands of vodka, such as Absolut and Stolichnaya, offer different flavorings that range from lemon to currant to pepper, and they can be ordered straight, on the rocks or in cocktails mixed with tonic water or any number of fruit juices. Grey Goose and Ketel One are the superior choices for devout metrosexuals.

Common Cocktails and the Men Who Love Them

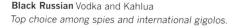

Mr. Gin and Tonic

Your choice of cocktail may reveal more about you than you realize. Of course, the confident man makes his own choices and is never swayed by stereotypes. Still, it never hurts to consider the message you may be sending.

Black Russian Vodka and Kahlua
Top choice among spies and international gigolos.

Cape Cod (aka vodka cranberry) Vodka and cranberry juice
Popular among body-conscious gym rats.

Daquiri Rum, lime juice and fruit mixer (served frozen)
Enjoyed by decorators and figure skaters.

Gin and Tonic On the rocks with a lime
A sensible choice for the educated man.

Greyhound Vodka and grapefruit juice
Good choice for the finicky, body-conscious gym rat.

Harvey Wallbanger Vodka, orange juice and Galliano
For goofy guys who are amused by goofy names.

Long Island Iced Tea Gin, rum, tequila, vodka, triple sec, sour mix and cola
College kids and amateurs only.

Madras Vodka, cranberry and orange juice
For prep school grads and polo types.

Manhattan Whiskey, sweet vermouth and bitters
Popular choice among grandfathers and lawyers.

Mai Tai Dark rum and pineapple juice
For the metro-man on a tropical holiday.

Margarita Tequila, sour mix and/or fresh lime juice (frozen or on
the rocks, with or without salt on the rim)
A good-time cocktail for a good-time guy.

Mojito Light rum, fresh mint leaves, lime and soda
An excellent summer choice for the debonair dude.

Rum and Coke Rum and cola
A dull choice for Dad.

Rusty Nail Scotch and Drambuie
For the manly man, but with a hint of the fancy.

Scotch Straight up, on the rocks, with water or soda
Very George Clooney.

Screwdriver Vodka and orange juice
An uninspired choice for the uninspired man.

Seabreeze Vodka, cranberry and grapefruit juice
Hello, Darling!

Sex on the Beach Vodka, cranberry juice, pineapple juice and
Peach Schnapps
For college guys who think it's funny.

Tequila Sunrise Tequila, orange juice and grenadine
A sweet choice for a man-child.

Tom Collins Gin, sour mix and a splash of soda
For professors and old queens.

Vodka Collins Vodka, sour mix and a splash of soda
See above.

Vodka Tonic On the rocks with a lime or lemon rind
Sensible and refreshing for the man who fears fruit.

White Russian Vodka, Kahlua and milk
For spies and international gigolos who dig dairy.

**Do Metrosexuals
Drink Beer?**
Yes they do. Of course,
European imports are
always preferable to
domestic brands.

Mr. Tom Collins

Hangovers

As a practical matter, there are several steps you can take to avoid the high price of a nasty hangover after your night of elegant debauchery. While there are certain preventative steps you can take in advance, others will require a minimum of coherence on your part before you collapse into bed.

- Never attend an important function on an empty stomach. Heinous stomach growls aside, you are far more likely to end up in the fountain with your pants around your ankles if you skip dinner. Don't count on hors d'oeuvres and nibbley bits to shield you from embarrassment.

- Keep a running count of your cocktails, and break up your rounds of drinks with a glass of water. If you've lost count, chances are your vocal volume is increasing and you're probably getting messy. If it's a big, debauched affair, and you're having fun, that's fine. Just remember, there may be photographers.

- Before you flop into bed, drink as much water as you possibly can. Hangovers are largely the result of dehydration, so make sure there's a full glass near your bedside when you wake up with your 90 lb. head in the morning.

Wine & Cocktails: The Bottom Line

Once you're out of college your days of beer bongs and keg parties should be behind you. There's nothing wrong with a good drink-up, but pacing yourself is essential. No one looks good falling ass-backwards over an ottoman.

I've had a wonderful time,...

...but this wasn't it. —Groucho Marx

3

Dining Out

Another arena where insecurities and self-consciousness can rear their ugly heads is in the world of restaurants. Though you may feel perfectly confident in the drive-thru, a finer restaurant is something else altogether. Even so, dining out need not be an occasion for angst if you simply comport yourself with dignity and avoid some common missteps.

Shall We Dine?

If restaurant etiquette is at all a mystery to you, the best thing to do is simply observe those around you. Bear in mind that observation is not staring, and subtlety is essential in such covert operations. Just remain relaxed, take your time and learn as you go.

Reservations and the Maitre d'

Most decent restaurants, whether casual or formal, attempt to orchestrate the seating of guests in order to avoid chaos and general disorder. Regardless of whether you are greeted by a waiter, a host or a maitre d', you should be gracious, friendly and relaxed, and you should not bum rush your table of choice.

If you have made reservations at a restaurant, simply introduce yourself by name. There is no need to bribe or surreptitiously slip the host or maitre d' money unless they have done you some special favor such as saving a special table or making special arrangements. If you are unhappy with the table offered to you, simply inform the host that you'd prefer to wait for another table.

If you are in a large group, it is considered good form to wait until all guests have arrived before disturbing the napkin arrangements, but if the other guests don't care, neither should you. If you find yourself seated at a round table and are confused by the settings, just remember that your glassware is to the right of your plate, and your bread plate is to the left.

Restaurant Dos and Don'ts

Do treat the maitre d' with respect.
Don't try to bribe him or call him *garçon*.

Do make yourself comfortable at the table.
Don't rearrange the furniture.

Do thank the maitre d' for seating you.
Don't slap him on the back.

Do wait for the waiter to approach your table.
Don't try to order from the maitre d'.

Do be aware of your surroundings at all times.
Don't hold the menu near a lit candle.

Do be aware of your surroundings at all times.

Enter the Waiter

Always greet your waiter in a friendly manner and allow him or her to tell you about the specials of the evening. When offered drinks or wine, ask your companions what they would like. If you order a bottle of wine, a good waiter will come by to refill the glasses for you throughout the course of the dinner.

Don't hold the menu near a lit candle.

Some restaurants, particularly French ones, offer "Prix Fixe" menus. These are meals that are served in several courses with a set price. Usually, there will be a choice of appetizers, entrees and desserts to choose from. You select one in each category, and a glass of wine or a cocktail may or may not be included.

Once you have decided what you'd like to order, close your menu to signal the waiter that you are ready. If you are hoping to impress, it is probably wise to avoid sloppy foods such as lobster, long pastas in tomato sauces or barbecued items, and remember that steaks and fish are best served medium-rare. Allow your guests to order first unless you have been asked to order for the table, and then see the waiter off with a smile and a thank you.

If you are on a date, you'll want to make an evening out of it and not rush toward the main course. Enjoy your appetizers and/or cocktails and take your time. Unless you are hurrying off to another event, dining out should be a leisurely and relaxed experience filled with conversation and interaction. This is true not only on dates, but also in groups, so slow down.

Salad Dressings

The finer the restaurant, the less likely you are to be offered a choice of salad dressings. That's what the chef does. He makes the perfect choice. If a selection of dressings is offered, the waiter will let you know. So, try to refrain from asking for Thousand Island dressing on your arugula salad.

Ordering Dos and Don'ts

Do signal for the waiter with a subtle wave of the hand.

Don't ever snap your fingers at the waiter.

Do signal for the waiter with a subtle wave of the hand.
Don't ever snap your fingers at the waiter.

Do feel free to ask the waiter for recommendations.
Don't ask, "What's good?"

Do inform the busser if you'd like water or bread.
Don't try to order drinks or dinner from the busser.

Do be respectful of the chef's creations in high-end restaurants.
Don't ask for ketchup.

Do remember that you are an adult.
Don't order milk.

Bon Appétit

As you are waiting for your meal, the waiter will most likely bring you a basket of bread to tide you over. In an Italian restaurant it may be served with a small plate of olive oil and herbs in which to dip the bread. Dip away, but be careful of dribbling. In a French restaurant it may come with a small tub of butter. In this case, use your knife to place a dab of butter on your bread plate, then tear off small pieces of your bread and butter them as you go.

Appetizers can be tricky as some may be eaten by hand and others should not be. Generally speaking, if it's at all possible to spear the item with a fork, then that's the way to go. Items served on toast or on a spear are finger foods, but, as always, when in doubt it's always best to wait and see what the others do.

When the main course arrives, the main thing to keep in mind is pacing. Enjoy your food, but also engage in the conversation. You don't want to devour your meal and end up sitting in front of an empty plate while everyone else is still eating. Additionally, it is wise to take small bites in the event that the conversation gets really good and you want to dive in. The last thing you want is to get caught with a huge mouthful when an intriguing question comes your way.

Do maintain your dignity.

Another thing to keep in mind is your use of silverware as you are eating. There is no need to clutch your knife and fork as if they will be stolen from you. Slice your food as you go and put your silverware down from time to time. Remember, used silverware should not be placed back on the tablecloth, but on the edge of your plate. And as previously mentioned, if you feel that you have something stuck in your teeth, do not attempt to rectify the situation at the table. Excuse yourself and perform the extraction in the bathroom.

Don't chew with your mouth open.

Dining Dos and Don'ts

Do maintain your dignity.
Don't chew with your mouth open.

Do swallow before speaking.
Don't speak with your mouth full.

Do wait a few moments if the food is too hot.
Don't blow on your food.

Do trust in the seasonings used by the chef.
Don't salt your food before trying it.

Do enjoy your meal and be yourself.
Don't tip backwards in your chair, burp or unbuckle your pants.

After-Dinner Coffee

While you may think your visits to Starbucks have fully enlightened you about the world of coffee, you may want to
think again. A nice restaurant is no place to be ordering a
frozen Frappuccino with sprinkles on top. It's best to stick to
one of the basics:

Espresso A dense coffee made by forcing steam through finely ground
coffee beans, always served black in small cups. (NOT pronounced
EX-presso.)

Cappuccino Espresso coffee mixed with hot, frothed milk or cream.
Often served with a pinch of chocolate powder or cinnamon on top.

Café Americano An espresso with hot water added.

Café Latte An espresso blended with unsteamed milk or cream.

Irish Coffee A coffee drink with Irish whiskey and whipped cream.

Mexican Coffee A coffee drink with Kahlua and a dollop of whipped
cream.

Check Please

Once the check has arrived, simply place your cash or credit card in the checkbook, close it and leave it at the edge of the table. In most situations, if the check is being split, it should be split evenly. Don't be the guy insisting that he's owed $2.75 in change. Even if you are the guest, or assume that someone else is paying, you should always have enough money to cover the situation in the event that you were mistaken.

If you are dining with a group and want to pick up the tab, you should excuse yourself discreetly and find your waiter early on in the evening. Give him your credit card and explain that you would like to pay the bill. This will prevent any tedious wrestling and debate when the check is delivered to the table.

A standard tip is between 15 and 20 percent of the total bill. Do not embarrass yourself by producing a calculator or tipping chart at the table. In most cities, just double the tax and add a few dollars if you had a nice time. As you leave you should thank the waiter and the maitre d'.

Kweezeen?

If the idea of a menu presented in a foreign language causes you to break out in a sweat, you might want to engage in a quick review of the terms listed on the next three pages before heading out the door. You don't need to memorize anything, but scanning the list will help you recognize a few items, and thus allow you to bluff a bit so you don't end up with a braised rabbit in raspberry sauce on your plate.

French Dining Glossary

Agnelle Lamb

Béarnaise An egg- and butter-based sauce with white wine

Beurre Butter

Bifteck Steak

Boeuf Beef

Bourguignonne Burgundy-style, cooked in red wine, bacon and onion

Champignons Mushrooms

Chou Cabbage

Consommé Clear soup

Coq Male chicken

Epinards Spinach

Escargot Land snail

Florentine With spinach

Foie Liver

Fromage Cheese

Hollandaise Egg yolk and butter sauce with lemon juice

Jambon Ham

Jus Juice

Lapin Rabbit (!)

Legumes Vegetables

Noix Nut

Oeuf Egg

Pain Bread

Poisson Fish

Pommes frites French fries

Potage Soup

Poulet Chicken (roasted)

Riz Rice

Rouille Tomato, pepper, olive oil and garlic paste

Sauce à vin Wine sauce

Steak frites Grilled steak with French-fried potatoes

Tomate Tomato

Veau Veal

Italian Dining Glossary

Affumicato Smoked

Aglio Garlic

Agnello Lamb

Alfredo Sauce made of cream and cheese

Arrabiatta Spicy tomato sauce with chilies and garlic

Arrosto Roast

Bistecca Steak

Bolognese Meat sauce (usually beef)

Carbonara Cream sauce with bacon and peas

Dolci Sweets, cakes

Formaggio Cheese

Forno, Al forno Roasted or baked

Fresco Fresh, uncooked, raw

Funghi Mushrooms

Gnocchi Bite-sized dumplings made of dough served in sauce

Griglia Broiled or grilled

Insalata (verde) Salad (green)

Manzo Beef

Marinara Traditional tomato sauce

Melanzane Eggplant

Olio Oil

Pancetta Bacon

Pesci Fish

Pomodoro Tomato sauce

Pollo Chicken

Primavera (Spring style) With vegetables

Prosciutto Italian ham

Puttanesca Tomato sauce with olives and capers

Risotto Rice

Tiramisu A sweet, layered dessert of sponge cake, cream, espresso and rum

Tortellini Curled pasta pieces stuffed with meat, cheese or vegetables

Vitello Veal

Zuppa Soup

Pastas

Capellini Long, thin, "angel hair" pasta

Farfalle Bow-tie pasta

Fettuccine Long, wide, flat pasta

Fusilli Spiral pasta

Penne Thin tubular pasta

Rigatoni Thick tubular pasta

Tagliolini Long, thin, flat pasta

Uh-oh, Sushi

Once considered an exotic delicacy, sushi is now a commonplace offering in restaurants around the world. While the mere idea of eating raw fish may leave the less adventurous feeling somewhat squeamish, any decent sushi bar will have a variety of fully cooked offerings, so that you can experiment at your own pace. Prepare to embrace the seaweed, and keep the following distinctions in mind as you scan the menu:

Sashimi Raw cuts of fish (tuna, salmon, etc.) that are served on their own for the true connoisseur. May be a bit too ambitious for the novice.

Nigiri Cuts of raw fish (occasionally cooked, as is freshwater eel) placed atop a small block of rice, and often held together by a strip of dried seaweed.

Maki Pieces of fish, crab or shrimp, often with cucumber or avocado, rolled into a tube of rice and seaweed, then sliced into bite-sized pieces. Vegetarian rolls are available for the truly cowardly.

Cones Similar to maki in that the fish, vegetables and rice are rolled in seaweed, but presented in the shape of an ice cream cone to be eaten by hand.

A note to the novice: The light green paste and pink shavings on the side are not guacamole and lox, but rather wasabi (similar to horseradish) and ginger. Do not try to eat these items on their own but rather as complements to be mixed in with your meal.

Dining In

Obviously there is a vast array of global cuisine out there just waiting to be discovered. Have you tried Vietnamese, Greek, Indian, Moroccan or Caribbean cuisine yet? In the end you may find that your true taste runs toward the basic comfort foods you grew up with. However, being open to experimentation will keep you learning and discovering at all times. And though eating out constantly may be beyond your budget, you can always try something new now and then.

A side benefit of experimenting with different culinary options is that you will be exposed to a greater variety of ingredients and spices that you might not otherwise encounter. Not only does this provide your digestive system and metabolism with a healthy workout, it will also ensure a wider variety of nutrients and vitamins in your diet. Eating the same foods all the time may sustain you, but it can also deprive you of proper nutrition.

It is always preferable to eat foods made from natural ingre-dients as opposed to the processed foods you may pick up at the supermarket. Even if you don't cook at home, try to get into the habit of buying real foods rather than prepackaged meals that come in boxes. Stick to the sides of the supermar-ket, and avoid the endless aisles of corporate cuisine. Keep your fridge full of cheeses, fruits, vegetables and juices, buy a few good spices and learn to broil a steak or a piece of fish at home. Snack on olives, nuts, bottled water and yogurt rather than bagged chips, soda and ice cream. You'll get used to it faster than you think, and you'll soon be rewarded with greater energy and a shrinking waistline.

Dining Out: The Bottom Line

Dining out should be a pleasant and enjoyable indulgence, but bad table manners are a major turnoff and can even be a deal breaker in business situations. So, relax, enjoy yourself and save your lustier instincts for the bedroom.

Every child is an artist....

...The problem is how to remain an artist
once he grows up. —Pablo Picasso

4

Art & Culture

To understand art is to recognize that from the earliest cave paintings, through ancient civilizations and medieval times, up until today, art has always reflected the cultural and societal evolution of humankind. People have always reacted strongly to that which is new and unexpected. Modern art (and it was all modern once) is often rejected as ugly or incomprehensible because, at its best, it is at the forefront of time and change. But with time, artwork slowly becomes less radical. Remember, there was a time when short skirts were scandalous, Elvis was evil, and the impish Andy Warhol was scary.

What the #*%@$?

That which is new is not always easily understood, and it usually provokes strong reactions on both sides. That's why each new generation seeks to find its new music, art and fashion in order to distinguish itself from the previous generation. Politics, sex and social change are always influencing art, and those who are unhappy with the latest societal shifts will most likely react negatively when the artistic mirror is held up to reflect those changes. Of course, not everything that is new is good or meaningful. Bad art, like bad music, literature and fashion, has always existed. But sometimes the larger movements and currents that shape the world can be captured in a single painting or sculpture.

So what is art? Art is created when a person manipulates any material in an intentional manner to evoke emotion or make a statement. And, how do you know when it's crap? You don't. But what you can do is open your mind and see if the artwork produces a reaction inside you. Does it relax you, irritate you, inspire you, make you feel tired, curious or horny? Good art gets a reaction. If it triggers your imagination, then it works for you on some level. With that in mind, your next trip to a museum or gallery should prove to be a lot more satisfying.

You don't need to be a scholar to enjoy art, and there is endless fascination to be found in those works of a bygone era. To be modern is to be in touch with the forward edge, but in order to understand what modern is, it is helpful to look backwards and understand the past.

Taking It All In

When visiting a world-class museum such as the Metropolitan in New York or the Louvre in Paris, it is simply not possible to take in everything in a single visit. Between the permanent collections and the traveling exhibitions, there is just too much to see, and trying to sweep through the place and see a bit of everything can only lead to disappointment. While it's nice to float around and browse, you should try to identify the two or three exhibitions that you are most curious about. Determine where they are and come up with a game plan.

Museum curators put a great deal of thought and planning into the layout of each exhibition. They are usually arranged with a beginning and an end in order to provide a logical context for the collection. Once you've decided what to see, take advantage of the planning and follow the progression. Oftentimes it will be a chronological sequence that explains the evolution of an artist or genre. Other times the works may be organized by subject matter. Whatever the case, remember that the works are not just randomly placed on the wall or scattered about the galleries. There is a story to each exhibition, and therein lies the interest.

Even in small galleries exhibiting a single collection of works, there are usually some copies of press clippings or reviews at the front desk to help you understand what you are seeing. Take your time and give each piece a good long look. Consider what you are looking at, notice the composition and think about your reaction. Then move on. Art is subjective, so you may find yourself entirely unimpressed by specific works or artists. But if that should happen, don't make the mistake of thinking that that is your reaction to all art. It's only your reaction to that artist or piece. Don't chuck in the towel. You wouldn't give up on music because you heard one lousy album.

Museum Dos and Don'ts

Do keep a respectful distance from the paintings.
Don't get too close and never touch anything.

Do keep a respectful distance from the paintings.

Don't get too close and never touch anything.

Do be aware of your surroundings.
Don't step in front of others and block their view.

Do take your time and consider individual works.
Don't rush through the exhibition, wondering why you don't get it.

Do keep your voice down.
Don't bellow out your opinions for all to hear.

Genres

The more you understand about a subject, the more interesting it becomes. This is true of sports, cars, cooking and astronomy. With that in mind, it won't hurt to take a very quick walk through some of the more significant eras of art history. At the very least, it will help you bluff your way through the conversation and recognize a few of the influences you find during your forays into the world of art.

The Renaissance Period

By 1425, the ancient Roman world was dead and a new age of ideas, vision, art and science was born. The Renaissance movement began in Italy and quickly spread across Europe, profoundly influencing the worlds of literature, science and art. It brought a rebirth of classical art, but with a new emphasis on anatomy, movement, expression, depth of field and scientific perspective. The big news was that art had become a three-dimensional, lifelike depiction of historical subjects and religious imagery. By the time the movement peaked in the early 1500s, the Flemish painters of the Netherlands had introduced landscapes and still lifes as subjects with a great deal of emphasis on light and shadows. The most famous examples of the era are Michelangelo's works inside the Vatican's Sistine Chapel and Leonardo da Vinci's *Mona Lisa*.

Masters

Leonardo da Vinci

Michelangelo

Raphael

Correggio

Botticelli

The Baroque Period

A term often used to refer to most art of the seventeenth century, the Baroque movement also began in Italy and spread to Austria, Germany and beyond. The style involved huge canvases featuring bright colors, extravagant flourishes and excessive grandeur with an emphasis on movement. Realism and religion were depicted in vivid, ornate detail. The grand Baroque style was favored by the Catholic Church for its public, religiously themed art, but by the mid 1600s private collectors began to demand smaller compositions suitable for private display. In the Netherlands, a group of painters that came to be known as the Dutch Masters began to sell their portraits, still lifes and landscapes to the wealthy middle classes rather than being commissioned by the church. In Spain, artists such as Diego Velázquez used light and shadow to achieve a harsh, new realism in the depiction of religious subjects. Two other styles of the seventeenth century to emerge were Classicism, which focused on the classical principles of art, and Naturalism, in which the lower-middle classes began to be depicted in taverns, kitchens and everyday situations.

Masters

Peter Paul Rubens

Diego Velázquez

Rembrandt van Rijn

Jan Vermeer

Rococo, Neoclassicism and Romanticism

In the eighteenth century, in the era of Louis XIV, three major styles of painting emerged. Rococo, which had grown out of the Baroque period, was full of excessively ornate flourishes with subjects that were very playful and hopelessly romantic. In the late 1700s, a more traditional, austere movement known as Neoclassicism emerged in France. Grand, historical themes and religious imagery made a comeback, with an emphasis on more formal techniques in which brushwork was less evident. By the early 1800s, during the Romantic period, artists began to incorporate deeper emotions, inner fears and the darker side of human psychology into their paintings. Rather than focusing exclusively on royal or historical figures, the life experience of the common man was central and things began to get more interesting.

Masters

Jacques-Louis David

Francisco Goya

Eugène Delacroix

Impressionism

By the 1860s a revolutionary new art movement had begun in France. In painting the landscapes of southern France and the leisured, Parisian middle classes, a group of cutting-edge artists began to experiment with short, abrupt brushstrokes that broke up the elements of light and color. When viewed at close range, the paintings seem chaotic and spotty, but when viewed from a distance the pictures became clearer as the colors and brushstrokes blended into an impressionistic whole. As photography emerged in the late 1800s, the art of painting had found itself a new and groundbreaking direction.

Masters

Edouard Manet

Claude Monet

Pierre-August Renoir

Edgar Degas

Expressionism

Though the term expressionism was not coined until the twentieth century, its roots can be traced back to the late 1800s. In an effort to move beyond the soft pastel colors and delicate textures of the impressionists, postimpressionist artists such as Vincent Van Gogh infused their work with greater emotional intensity, bolder colors and more impulsive, thicker brushwork. The results were far more dramatic works that were often distorted, intense and even childlike. The emotions of the artist began to take center stage from the subject matter, and reactions to the aggressive new style of painting were far from universally positive in the beginning.

Masters

Vincent Van Gogh

Edvard Munch

Paul Cézanne

Henri Matisse

Paul Gauguin

Cubism and Surrealism

By the early twentieth century a variety of influences from the modern industrial era had found their way into the world of art. Cubism was a simplification of forms in which geometric shapes and unexpected colors were used to symbolize the artist's subject matter. Cubists altered the relationship of time and space, and fragments became finished products. It was the age of Freud and artists such as Picasso were inspired to explore deeper realms of the psyche through artistic expression. Deliberate distortion and bold brushwork pushed the envelope as artists continued to reveal their innermost thoughts and impulses in an entirely new and modern way. The subconscious had been unleashed upon the canvas, and eventually the Surrealist movement emerged in which artists, including Salvador Dali, depicted dream states, hallucinations, fantasy and even absurdism. It was the beginning of modern and pop art as we know it today.

Masters

Pablo Picasso

Georges Braque

Joan Miró

Salvador Dali

Sex, Sex, Sex!

If you got bored and skipped over the previous section, go back and read it! You should know this stuff, and the paragraphs could not possibly be any shorter, for God's sake.

The Masters

While the pantheon of great historical artists is a vast one, there are certain names that have been elevated over time to iconic status. These are the names recognized by the masses, even if their individual histories are unfamiliar to most. To help place them in time and to grasp the essence of their contributions, here's a quick review:

Leonardo da Vinci (1452-1519) Born outside of Florence, Italy, Leonardo was a trained painter who traveled throughout Italy establishing himself as a true master. His works inspired an entire generation of Italian artists, including Michelangelo, Botticelli and Raphael. A true genius, he created hundreds of inventions and even drew plans for a flying machine. His best-known masterpieces are the *Mona Lisa* and *The Last Supper.*

Michelangelo (1475-1564) Born Michelangelo Buonarroti in Caprese, Italy, he is today one of the most revered figures in art history. Known for his marble sculptures and exquisite paintings, many of his works were commissioned by the Roman Catholic Church and deal with religious imagery. He was also an accomplished architect and poet, and unlike so many other artists, he achieved great fame in his lifetime. Among his most famous works are the frescoes on the ceiling of the Sistine Chapel and *The Last Judgment,* and the sculptures *Pietà* and *David.*

Rembrandt van Rijn (1606-1669) The greatest artist to emerge from the Netherlands, Rembrandt was born in the town of Leiden. Known for his use of light and shadow, warm colors and his ability to convey the inner life of his subjects, he produced hundreds of paintings in his lifetime, including roughly a hundred self-portraits. In recent years it has been found that some of his lesser-known drawings and paintings may have been the works of his students, but that has done nothing to diminish his impact. *The Night Watch* and *The Return of the Prodigal Son* are considered to be two of his greatest masterpieces.

Claude Monet (1840–1926) Born in Paris, the master impressionist is perhaps best known for his landscapes set in the French countryside and his idyllic scenes of the French middle classes. Much of his work is identifiable by his use of soft pastel colors favoring purples, oranges, blues and greens. His fascination with outdoor light led him to paint several series of paintings depicting the same scene in various stages of daylight. Among his most famous works are *Water Lilies*, the *Haystack* series, and *Women in the Garden*.

Pierre-August Renoir (1841–1919) Born in Limoges, France, Renoir was an impressionist, but unlike Monet, he preferred figure painting to landscapes, and he often used his wife and children as models. His paintings were often bright, sunny and lively depictions of family life in the parks and gardens of Paris. Additionally, his numerous studies of the female nude form are considered to be works of great beauty. *The Swing, The Luncheon of the Boating Party* and the series *The Bathers* are among his better-known works.

Vincent van Gogh (1853–1890) The famously tormented Dutchman who sold just one painting in his lifetime was born in Groot-Zundert, the

Netherlands. In his early thirties, he moved to Paris to live with his brother Théo, an art dealer, and it was there that he met many famous artists of the day. He eventually moved to southern France, where he produced his most famous works, including *Starry Night, Sunflowers* and *Bedroom at Arles*. During his later years, van Gogh battled mental illness and was repeatedly hospitalized, but between the bouts of madness he produced an astonishing number of vivid, emotional paintings with his trademark swirling brushstrokes, often in bright blues, greens and yellows. Eventually overcome by the agony of his mental state, he took his own life with a revolver. Today his works are considered masterpieces of expressionism.

Pablo Picasso (1881–1973) Perhaps the most original and influential artist of the twentieth century, Picasso was born in Malaga, Spain, but lived most of his life in France. Throughout his career he experimented with a variety of styles. His truly original style first emerged during his famed Blue Period (1901–1904) in which he worked only in shades of blue depicting solitary, melancholy figures. His subsequent period focused largely on circus performers and came to be known as his Rose Period (1904–1906). In 1907 he painted *Les Demoiselles d'Avignon*, which is widely regarded as the birth of Cubism. The depiction of five female nude figures in sharp, fragmented, geometric shapes changed the course of art forever. Thirty years later he painted *Guernica*, a bold condemnation of fascism and war. His truly unique and ever-evolving body of work is instantly recognizable the world over. To this day his work elicits mixed reactions, but his embrace of chaos and complete disregard for the accepted rules of art made him a world-class rebel and the father of modern art.

Your Own Creativity

Some men are graced with inherent artistic abilities, while others have trouble drawing a straight line. Wherever your own abilities and strengths may lie, the more art you expose yourself to, the more you may find yourself compelled to express your own creativity. This is an impulse and an opportunity you should pay attention to.

The Zen-like process of expressing yourself through art can be highly satisfying. And it doesn't require a silly smock, a beret or an easel in the living room. Exploring your own art is another way of expressing your personal style. And that art may take the form of painting, photography, writing, web design, cooking, woodwork, car restoration or any other form imaginable. The idea is to explore your potential and develop your interests. Producing a masterpiece is not the goal. Discovering something new, enjoying the artistic process and expanding your horizons is the objective.

Art & Culture: The Bottom Line

Cheesy art provides answers.
Great art poses questions.

Real knowledge...

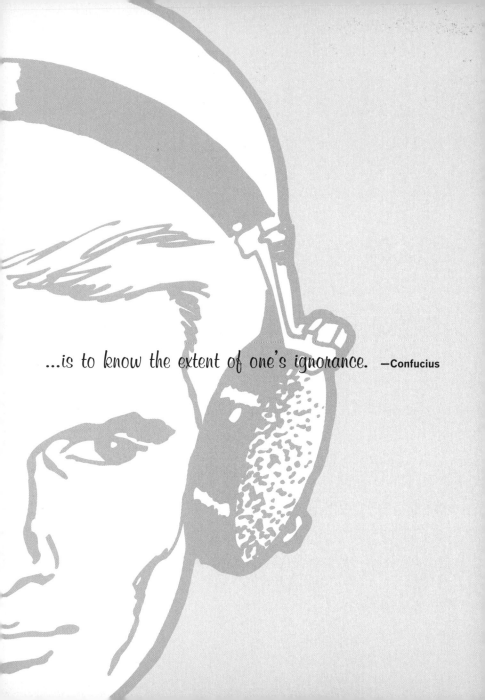

...is to know the extent of one's ignorance. —Confucius

5

Music, Books & Film

It is said that we are the sum of our experiences. While that may be true, there's no reason we can't steal from the lives of others. Books, films and music provide infinite opportunities to walk in the shoes of another, to understand new ideas and to discover the universe beyond our own little corner of the world. Whether you're living in a New York penthouse or holed up in a cozy little trailer by the sea, the world is at your fingertips and it's your responsibility to explore it.

Beyond the Obvious

No matter where you are or what your limitations might be, there is life beyond television. Sitcoms and reality TV may be a welcome escape from life's troubles, twenty-four-hour news coverage may keep you informed of politics and global issues, and an ever-increasing selection of cable channels sometimes offers fascinating scientific or historic documentaries that can be very eye-opening. Still it is called television *programming* for a reason. So, unless you're happy with the idea of being a pajama-clad robot programmed to laugh, learn and vote, you may want to seek out some other influences.

At their best, literature, music and cinema are open to individual interpretation, and therein lies one of their essential values. Ideas are presented in an artistic context for you to digest and evaluate on your own. It isn't always easy to find the great works amid the sea of cultural dreck, but the variety of books you read, the music you listen to and the films you see are an integral part of what makes your life experience unique. They mark the difference between a person who can have a conversation and a person who just repeats the jokes and opinions he saw on television; the difference between a metrosexual man of style and an uninformed couch potato.

Musical Ambience

Hopefully, by this point in life you have emerged from your head-banger phase and are open to some more varied musical options. If not, just play along. You see, the music that you surround yourself with can be considered the soundtrack to your life, and whether you are lounging at home, throwing a party or seducing a gorgeous little number in your love nest, ambience counts.

Temporary obsessions, new discoveries and guilty pop pleasures are part of everyone's existence and make life fun and varied. Therefore, you should never question your own tastes and you should enjoy whatever music floats your boat. But beyond the angry anthems of hostile young men and the fluffy confections thrust upon the world by ex-Mouseketeers, there is a world of music out there, both old and new, so keep your ears open.

As you age, you may find that you are less and less interested in the commercially packaged trends churned out by record companies and publicity machines. This is not a sign that you are over the hill, it is a sign that your musical tastes are evolving and your personal style has found yet another outlet through which to exhibit itself. This is a good thing. The less programmed you become by pop culture, the more you will begin to recognize the value of the music that speaks to you, and the more inclined you will be to experiment.

Make a point of getting tickets next time your latest musical discovery is in town. Invite a friend to have cocktails at a jazz bar rather than your usual watering hole, or impress a date with an evening of classical music in the park. Just get out there and try something new. You may not always love what you hear, but you'll be broadening your perspective and you'll have something to talk about at cocktail parties or on your next date.

Music can lift your spirits, calm you down, inspire creativity or add a sultry backdrop to a sexually charged scenario. At home, music is always a good alternative to television as it focuses you on your own life rather than on the lives of others. House cleaning is always a lot more entertaining with Grace Jones purring "Pull Up to the Bumper" in the background, and you're more likely to balance your checkbook or plot your course for world domination if you aren't hypnotized by the small screen.

Fifteen Albums You Should Own

Your personal music library says a lot about who you are. Don't pretend to like things that you don't. That's pointless. But the more music you expose yourself to, the more likely you are to find a variety of music that really speaks to you. And you can always sell back the duds. Here are a few suggestions that might be worth adding to your collection:

- *Buena Vista Social Club*—Ry Cooder
- *Chet Baker in Paris*—Chet Baker
- *What's Goin' On*—Marvin Gaye
- *Du Jazz Dans Le Ravin*—Serge Gainsbourg
- *Best of Sade (Remastered)*—Sade
- *The Mission: Soundtrack*—Ennio Morricone
- *Painted from Memory*—Elvis Costello and Burt Bacharach
- *Blue Lines*—Massive Attack
- *Four Sider*—Sergio Mendes & Brasil '66
- *The Moderns: Soundtrack*—Mark Isham
- *Speaking in Tongues*—Talking Heads
- *Best of Bowie*—David Bowie
- *Vertigo*—Groove Armada
- *Parachutes*—Coldplay
- *Berlin*—Lou Reed

Five Music Icons for the Metrosexual Man

David Bowie Because he was fearless in pushing the envelope not only musically, but in terms of theatricality, androgyny and mystery.

Jim Morrison Because of his unbridled sexuality, his poetry, his independence and his ability to pull off leather pants.

Sting Because he went from school teacher to pop star, created a musical style all his own, embraced yoga and tantric sex and remains relevant and ageless.

Marvin Gaye Because he was quietly and smoothly seductive, always looked sharp and infused his singing with strength, sexuality and vulnerability.

Mick Jagger Because he challenged traditional ideas of masculine beauty, he has seen it all and he is both a rock star and a man of the manor.

Movies vs. Films

What is the difference between movies and films? In reality the two terms are interchangeable, but to many the distinction between the two is an important one. You might say that while movies are beer, films are wine. Beer is easily consumed, fun to indulge in and comes in a variety of brands. There are light beers, dark beers, cheap beers and top-of-the-line beers. Wine is more complex and is more of an acquired taste. Defined by region and produced with a much greater attention to detail, wines are multifaceted and contain subtleties and distinctions that are not always immediately recognizable. Of course, there are also cheap wines. So it is with the two realms of the cinema.

This is not to say that one is superior to the other, as both serve their purpose. But generally speaking, movies tend to follow more traditional story arcs with linear narratives and clearly defined heroes and villains. Films tend to be more character-driven and provide a much narrower and more focused point of view. Hollywood blockbusters are often made by committee and are tailored to suit the expectations of a general audience, while films tend to reflect the personal vision of the filmmaker.

To some, the idea of an "art" film conjures up images of pretentious, self-indulgent blather and tedious, sleep-inducing symbolism. In many cases, that estimation is entirely accurate. However, as in any art form, there are brilliant works out there just waiting to be discovered. While some can be hilariously funny, others may be quietly profound. But the most satisfying films are those that take you into another world, provide you with a new perspective and inspire reflection. Great movies can also achieve these same goals.

The world of cinema offers infinite opportunities to learn, experience and broaden one's horizons. The idea is not to limit yourself to a single genre, but to be open to the entire spectrum. Do not tune out prematurely to that which is unfamiliar. All films require a willing suspension of disbelief, and even those whose deeper meanings escape you at first can still leave a lasting impression. Of course, as in all aspects of life, crap is unavoidable. However, an open mind and a willingness to experiment can result in some fantastic surprises. It's just like sex.

Fifteen Films You Should See

The following fifteen films—listed in no particular order—are all worth seeing, and each for different reasons. Some are about visual imagery and poetry, some explore themes regarding the meaning of life and some are just flat-out, stylized fun. You figure it out. And pay attention to the directors. Every one of them is worth exploring further if you like what you see.

- *La Dolce Vita*—Federico Fellini
- *Fargo*—The Coen Brothers
- *The Elephant Man*—David Lynch

- *Cinema Paradiso*—Giuseppe Tornatore
- *The Last Emperor*—Bernardo Bertolucci
- *A Clockwork Orange*—Stanley Kubrick
- *Tie Me Up, Tie Me Down*—Pedro Almodovar
- *Wings of Desire*—Wim Wenders
- *Amélie*—Jean-Pierre Feunet
- *Brazil*—Terry Gilliam
- *The Remains of the Day*—James Ivory
- *American Beauty*—Sam Mendes
- *Cabaret*—Bob Fosse
- *Koyaanisqatsi*—Godfrey Reggio
- *Sunset Boulevard*—Billy Wilder

Five Film Icons for the Metrosexual Man

Cary Grant Because he defined sophistication for his generation, he undercut his suave persona with a sense of humor and he rose from the bottom to the top.

James Dean Because he was a world-class rebel, he revealed his soul in an era of buttoned-down conservatism and he became a legend.

Marlon Brando Because back in the day he exuded animal magnetism on the screen, he was a master at his craft and he made torn T-shirts and sulking sexy.

Paul Newman Because he portrays strength and dignity onscreen and always looks fantastic doing it, he is both adventurous and charitable and he is ultimately ageless.

Steve McQueen Because he proved that supreme masculinity and high style are not mutually exclusive, he lived his life through his art and he looked great in a turtleneck.

Night Table Reading

There is no person on earth who has read everything. In fact, there are many who have read nothing. Avoid those people. In any case, a good book on the nightstand is essential for any man wishing to improve himself. Whether you have a preference for biographies, novels, nonfiction or light, comedic fluff, reading should be an entertaining endeavor that you look forward to. The key is to find the right book.

It never hurts to have read a few classics. *War and Peace* may be a bit ambitious, but you'll be doing yourself a big favor if you get yourself up to speed on a few of those titles you skipped over in school. Start with those titles that everyone is always referring to that leave you feeling clueless. It's worth the effort. Chances are if a book is revered as a classic, there must be something worthwhile in it, and it's surely in paperback so you can always chuck it out if it turns out to be a big yawn.

Ask friends and associates for suggestions. Spend an hour just poking around in a bookstore. You'll find something, and maybe pique your interest in other subjects. Pick up three books and get around to them when you can—on the train, on vacation, in bed at night. At least you'll have them lying around, so you can chip away at them slowly and people can see how literate you are.

Fifteen Books You Should Read

Though you may have a particular area of interest or a favorite genre, it is important to mix things up and expose yourself to different voices and writing styles. Some books may shock and surprise you through humor, darkness, or deliberate frankness. Others may simply transport you to distant places where characters lead extraordinary lives. Take 'em or leave 'em:

- *The Great Gatsby* by F. Scott Fitzgerald
- *The Sun Also Rises* by Ernest Hemingway
- *Myra Breckenridge* by Gore Vidal
- *The Turn of the Screw* by Henry James
- *Things Fall Apart* by Chinua Achebe
- *Underworld* by Don DeLillo
- *Maus* and *Maus II* by Art Spiegelman
- *Perfume* by Patrick Susskind
- *On the Road* by Jack Kerouac
- *The Stranger* by Albert Camus
- *Love in the Time of Cholera* by Gabriel García Márquez
- *The Berlin Stories* by Christopher Isherwood
- *The Unbearable Lightness of Being* by Milan Kundera
- *Barrel Fever* by David Sedaris
- *Fight Club* by Chuck Palahniuk

Music, Books & Film: The Bottom Line

You are responsible for your own education, and the books, movies and music you expose yourself to become a part of who you are. Become interested and you will become interesting.

Art produces ugly things
which frequently become more beautiful with time....

...Fashion, on the other hand, produces beautiful things which always become ugly with time. —Jean Cocteau

6

Fashion & Personal Style

Throughout the ages, in all societies, fashion has served as an indicator of social status and cultural belonging. From the Masai tribes of Kenya and Tanzania to the upper classes of Britain and Japan, the way people dress proclaims their place in a given society. To know one's uniform is to fit into the social hierarchy.

The Function of Fashion

Military uniforms provide a clear indication of power, status and rank. To adopt a uniform is to state that, "I think like you, and I am one of you." This principle filters all the way down to sports fans wearing cheese-hats or sports jerseys to indicate their alliances. In politics, heads of state will deliberately alter their appearance when dealing with foreign cultures. Eastern leaders may abandon their traditional garb in favor of a Western-style suit when visiting and negotiating with a Western nation. Similarly, U.S. politicians carefully calibrate their wardrobes to establish a link with a particular audience. They'll wear jeans and a windbreaker to address the coal miners of Kentucky, a conservative business suit to glad-hand their corporate donors and a tuxedo to mingle with the power elite of Hollywood.

Perhaps the greatest example of the power of appearance occurred during the televised 1960 presidential debates between John F. Kennedy and Richard Nixon. Kennedy looked youthful, tanned and relaxed in his slim-cut suit. Nixon had a five o'clock shadow, looked rumpled and perspired throughout the debate. After the debates, polls indicated that those who had listened on the radio overwhelmingly thought that Nixon had come out on top. But among those who saw the debates on television, the vast majority felt that Kennedy had done a far superior job. And we all know how that election turned out.

Of course, on the other side of the equation, making a unique fashion statement says, "I am not like you." By rejecting standard conventions, whether subtly or blatantly, a man can set himself apart from the masses and proclaim his individuality. If you want to be the Midnight Cowboy, go for it. The key lies in making the decision consciously rather than simply dressing obnoxiously to draw attention to yourself. In the final analysis, however, it is far more impressive to express your sense of style through small touches as opposed to garish choices.

Avoiding Ridicule

In the ever-changing world of fashion, it takes a lot of energy to keep pace. You can look to a celebrity you admire for inspiration, you can flip through the fashion rags for ideas or you can seek out a designer label or clothing line that generally works for you. The key is to identify which styles look best on you and then find variety within those guidelines.

However you choose to develop your personal style, it is essential that you maintain a realistic grasp of your body type. Thin men can wear tight-fitting styles that fat men cannot. Tall men can wear looser clothes that short men cannot. And very few men can pull off sheer shirts, leather pants and fur. You already know if you are one of those men.

Similarly, it is important to remember to always dress your age. Nothing looks more tragic than a forty-year-old man dressed like a hip-hop, skate rat. This is not to imply that fashion is only for the young. On the contrary, a fashionable appearance will work in your favor for your entire life. Again, first impressions are lasting ones, and to dismiss fashion and personal style as frivolous indulgence is a big mistake. Regardless of your profession or economic status, people will always respond more positively to a man who is self-aware and well dressed. Catch their eye, and you've caught their attention.

Don't Even Think About It!

So, you're ready to dress your age, and you're going to choose your wardrobe based on the reality of your body type. That's great. But before you create your new self, you may want to review the following list of unforgivable crimes. If you have been guilty of any of these, do not tell anyone. Keep it to yourself, pack up a bag and leave it on the front steps of the nearest charity shop. You'll be doing yourself a huge favor if you avoid:

Avoid cowboy hats.

Avoid pleated or pre-cuffed jeans.

- Cowboy hats (they're over)
- Varsity jackets
- Colorful vests
- Christmas sweaters
- Bolo ties
- Pleated or pre-cuffed jeans
- Acid-washed anything
- Ties with short sleeves
- Mesh anything
- Cropped pants
- Hot pants
- Gym socks with shoes
- Boots with shorts
- Platform shoes
- Tatty underwear

Getting It Right

If you want to rebuild your wardrobe but aren't sure where to begin, just remember that if your clothes are well cut and simple in design, you can make strong statements with a few crucial accessories. Bad jewelry is sure to elicit chuckles, so be careful and keep it to a minimum, and be aware that your shoes, your watch and your belt will say more about you than you may realize. Of course, this is also true of ill-fitting pants, a rumpled shirt and a goofy blazer. As you set about rebuilding your wardrobe, bear the following rules of thumb in mind:

- Your safest bet is to stick to solid colors, darker tones and clean lines for your basic wardrobe items.
- Pirate shirts, loud patterns, buckles and zippers are for circus performers and boy bands.
- Pleated pants are history. Slim-fit, straight-leg pants make you look longer and sharper.
- Shorter, stouter men should avoid double-breasted jackets. Single-breasted lapels add length and line.
- Dress shirts should be 100% cotton and should be professionally laundered. Have them hung on hangers rather than folded to avoid creases.
- Wearing the right size is essential. Your clothes should conform to your body. If an article of clothing is too tight or too loose, the whole look is blown.
- If your pants are too long or your suit is too boxy, spend a few dollars on alterations. It's not expensive and you'll look much better.
- Your belt and your shoes should always match, and black on black works best.
- Suspenders should be avoided, but if you absolutely must wear them, only wear them with a suit, and never with a belt.
- Eyeglasses can make a great style statement, or an idiotic one, so choose wisely. Avoid brightly colored eyewear and always get a second opinion.
- A silver, stainless-steel watchband will go with everything. Leather bands should be strong and masculine, and sport watches are for sporting occasions.
- High school or college rings are best kept in the dresser drawer until the reunion is announced.

In or Out?
As a general rule, dress shirts should be tucked in, and casual shirts should be worn untucked.

- Rings and bracelets, if you are so inclined, need to work with your watch and belt, and should always be kept to a minimum. They can work if you don't mix metals.
- Necklaces made of leather cord or beads should only be worn with t-shirts or casual, open-neck, long-sleeved shirts.
- Chain necklaces should not be too thin or too long, and should never be left hanging outside your shirt unless you're featuring serious ice. (Diamonds, that is, and, well . . . don't wear diamonds.)
- Cufflinks are an elegant touch but should only be worn with dress shirts and preferably with French cuffs.
- A slim billfold or money clip is important, as a bulging wallet will only produce unsightly lumps in all the wrong places.

Ten Wardrobe Must-Haves

Look Before You Leap
Shopping without buying is the best way to cultivate your fashion savvy and tap into current trends. It also cuts down on regrettable impulse purchases.

Your personal wardrobe should always be evolving. The general rule is that you should throw out, or donate to charity, anything you haven't worn in the last two years. The key is downsizing. Lose the frumpy, sentimental stuff, and change with the times. Keep the T-shirt you love, but lose the reindeer sweater your mother bought you back when you were tragic. In the final analysis, the perfect male wardrobe is infinitely— and thankfully—less complicated than the female wardrobe. Obviously, you need to find what works for you, but here are ten elements that you really shouldn't be without:

- Three black T-shirts, three new white T-shirts
- Two different pairs of flattering jeans
- One dark suit
- One leather or suede short coat (not a bomber jacket)
- Two rollneck or crewneck cable-knit sweaters
- Two pairs of dark, straight-leg, nonpleated pants

- Three well-cut, solid-color, button-down shirts (one white)
- Quality sunglasses
- One expensive watch, one sports watch
- Flattering underwear

Designer Labels

If you've got a little extra cash to spend, investing in a small selection of great items can make a huge difference in your wardrobe. It isn't necessary to dress in one look from head to toe, in fact, a few good pieces can be mixed with simple wardrobe staples to create your own individual style. If you can only afford a few items, go with solid colors that you can wear in a variety of combinations. Loud, bright items grow old quickly and you don't want people saying, "Oh, that looks good on you . . . again."

Kenneth Cole Great shoes and outerwear, clean masculine lines and subdued colors and prints. Good for professionals and ageless men.

Armani Classic Italian tailoring, usually understated, but always a safe bet. From tuxedoes to T-shirts, Armani provides consistent quality pieces.

Gucci Very slick and stylish, often sexy and dangerous. Gucci conveys luxury with a touch of decadence. Beautiful suits for anyone, and fantastic sunglasses and other accessories if you can pull them off.

Donna Karan Great casuals and outerwear, understated, relaxed elegance for all body types. Particularly good sweaters and shirts, with a consistent feeling to the design. Ageless appeal.

Ralph Lauren Classic style for a Newport/Hamptons vibe. Easy to mix and match casuals for the modest metrosexual who still wants a strong look. Absolute tops if you're going boating.

Dolce & Gabbana Surprisingly elegant suits and casual wear that ranges from daring to outrageous. The bolder, flashier pieces are favored by models and movie stars, so you'd better look like one of the two if you're going to try and pull them off.

Helmut Lang Austrian techno-chic for those with an architectural eye. Sometimes avant-garde, but lots of great slim-line pieces that can really add subtle style to simple ensembles.

Prada Famously geared toward the thin man, the fashion-forward Prada style is known for distinct prints, narrow cuts and high price tags. A very stylish label and an excellent line of shoes considered must-haves by footwear connoisseurs.

Calvin Klein Famous for the underwear, Klein also offers relatively conservative choices in everything from suits to sportswear. Always a safe bet for those with more conservative inclinations.

Versace The ultimate in Italian flamboyance. The often over-the-top styles are best left to those who seek maximum attention, though it doesn't hurt for every man to have something loud for loud occasions.

John Varvatos A handsome, tasteful line with beautiful, quality suedes and sweaters. A good choice for any age and body type as the looks tend to be understated yet still very stylish.

Sean John Urban chic for the young and brash. Primarily youth-oriented, but with some surprisingly well-tailored, classic pieces in the mix. Ideal for the young, urban athlete, but not the best choice for the more mature metro man.

Y-3 A brand new label pairing designer Yohji Yamamoto with the Adidas line. Very twenty-first century, progressive sportswear utilizing the familiar three stripes in new ways. Sometimes over the top, but some of the simpler pieces are great.

Wardrobe Staples

It isn't necessary to own a closetful of designer duds to look good on a day-to-day basis. The trick is to stock up on basic staples that you can mix in with your high-end purchases. Needless to say, it's essential to keep your underwear and sock drawers well-stocked and frequently updated as there is nothing so unforgivable as ratty underpants or old socks. The age-old debate between boxers and briefs has become somewhat passé as there are now a variety of styles in men's underwear. The choice is yours, though your selection should depend not solely on comfort, but also on which style is most flattering to your body type as you saunter across the bedroom toward your intended. The combo boxer-brief makes for clean lines under a suit, while the thong remains primarily a source of comedy.

The other staples in your wardrobe should include a variety of T-shirts, solid color sweaters, jeans and casual pants that can be mixed and matched with your more impressive jackets, shirts, shoes and other designer items. These staples can be inexpensive purchases, but should not under any circumstances include pocket-tees or pleated khakis. Again, dark and neutral colors are best for these staples so that they can be worn frequently without drawing attention to themselves or competing with your finer items. The following chain stores carry good-quality staples at affordable prices, so you can stock up on basic T-shirts, sweaters, shirts and pants for everyday wear:

The Gap Good for the most basic of all staples. Low-priced, ultra-casual sportswear, T-shirts, sweaters, shorts and basics pants to knock around in on the weekend.

Banana Republic Affordable basics for the office and casual dress situations. Look for the narrow-cut poplin shirts, straight-leg pants, long-sleeved tees, sweaters and some decent outerwear.

J. Crew Selections range from beachwear to suits and shoes with a tendency toward the preppy aesthetic. Some nice, subdued slacks, sweaters and accessories can be found amid the more colorful items.

Club Monaco Great staples with a touch more of the European aesthetic than The Gap or J. Crew. Slim lines, solid colors and stylish prints offer variety with small touches that add a bit of extra style. Good for mixing in with your higher-end items.

H & M Amazing bargains can be found at the stores of this international retailer based in Sweden. A great place to pick up quality pieces with a nice European influence that sets them apart from the U.S. brands. You may have to look through some cheaper stuff to get to the good, but the killer prices make it well worth the effort.

**Small Touches—
Big Impact**

It is far better to invest in quality accessories to dress up a simple outfit than to wear expensive clothes with cheap accessories.

Shoes: The Ultimate Giveaway

One of the great mysteries of the 1970s was how the doormen at Studio 54, that ultimate fortress of exclusivity, decided who would be let in and who would spend the evening on the pavement. It has since been revealed that one of the deciding factors in borderline cases was a quick look at the shoes. A great-looking guy with the right attitude and all the right clothes could be completely undone by a pair of dirty, white sneakers. Times may have changed, but certain things still hold true. Your shoes still give you away. So at the very least, be sure you've got the following:

• At least two pairs of versatile, black shoes that can be worn with jeans as well as a dark suit. That means they need to fall somewhere between combat boots and shiny, lace-up, executive shoes. Regardless of whether you choose Doc Martens or $400 Pradas, you should avoid anything too trendy as the shoes should not draw attention to themselves. Spend the time and the money to find the right ones, so you can step out in confidence every time.

- Sneakers still have their place in society, especially since professional sports have elevated athletic gear to the realm of high fashion. Get a good pair you can wear to the gym, and one stylish pair, from lines like Diesel or Puma, that you can wear out at night if the setting is right and you're going for the blasé sports-star look.

- One sturdy, masculine pair of sandals. Worn in the heat of summer with shorts or jeans, it's a great, laid-back look. We're not talking about beachwear here, so avoid those nylon numbers with neon labels and go for dark leather. (Don't even think about socks.)

Remember that these are only the basics. Your job, your lifestyle and your social life will surely require more than five pairs of shoes, but if you've got the basics in place, you're unlikely to experience that sinking feeling of doom when all the pretty people are staring at your feet in horror. Think of your shoes as a worthwhile investment, and treat them as such by keeping them in good shape.

Colors

Generally speaking, cool, dark colors such as black, gray and navy blue are safe bets for most men, especially in professional situations. Warmer, brighter colors can look great as well, but should be chosen carefully, and really loud, obnoxious colors are for really loud, obnoxious men. Pay attention to what you're wearing when you get compliments. It might be the style, but it might also be the color. Conversely, if people blanche and turn away when you show up in your tangerine blouse, it might be time for another trip to the charity shop.

Though finding the right colors for you often requires a bit of experimentation, you shouldn't be shy about asking friends or salespeople for their opinions. Also, bear in mind that wearing certain colors can send subliminal signals in the workplace or in romantic situations. Sure, this is very subtle stuff, but it's worth paying attention to:

Red Considered the warmest, sexiest and most passionate color. Always good on a date to throw in a little red, and in business situations, a red tie can signal boldness and confidence.

Blue The calmest of all colors can be used to project a calm and approachable feeling. Dark blues indicate solid strength, while lighter shades come across as friendly.

Green Bright greens don't look good on many people, but darker shades can be a nice alternative to too much blue. A comfortable choice for casual situations.

Yellow While yellow is a "warm and happy" color, it looks terrible on most men, so be careful. It's fine for those with darker skin tones, but anyone else should get a second opinion.

Purple The color of royalty, purple is best in small doses. Sometimes nice for ties or pinstripes on shirts, but generally speaking, too much purple is just too much.

Orange Risky business. Sweaters in rusty shades can look good on dark-haired men, but bright orange is rarely a good choice unless you're deeply tanned and holding a Mai Tai.

Brown Earthy and masculine, browns usually look quite handsome on most men, but mid-range shades are not always the best choice for really fair-skinned guys. For maximum impact it's best to go with very deep, dark shades.

Gray Deep charcoal grays are great for suits and sweaters and can be very flattering, but lighter grays can make some men look washed out and bland. Still, they go with almost any other color so they're a fairly safe bet.

Black The great equalizer no man should be without, black conveys power, confidence and a little bit of danger. Appropriate for almost any situation, it's a must-have for every man's wardrobe.

Formal Dress

Formal affairs can be problematic if you don't understand what exactly is being called for. Invitations that indicate a dress code are not meant to intimidate, but to save you from embarrassing yourself. It is fair warning that a lot of effort and planning is being put into the event, and your effort in dressing the part will be appreciated.

If you can afford to buy a nice, tailored tuxedo, that's great. Go for a simple, classic black one with a minimum of fussy details. Too much satin, funky lapels or excessive ruffles will only look silly and dated in a short period of time. If you don't feel a tuxedo is a worthwhile investment for you, you should consider a classic black suit. If worn with a straight-collar white shirt and solid, black tie (straight or bow), it is a perfectly acceptable alternative to a tuxedo.

The great thing about the classic, black suit is that it can also look sexy with an open collar for more casual affairs, or be worn with a tie for business. In any case, you'll always feel more comfortable in a suit of your own than in a rental. Now, regarding those dress codes for formal affairs, here's the breakdown:

Casual No tie is required, but you still need to dress nicely. A jacket or suit is optional.

Semi-Formal Best to go with a dark suit and black shoes.

Black Tie Optional A semi-formal affair at which either a dark suit or a tuxedo is acceptable. When given the option, you'll look cooler with a nice, dark suit.

Black Tie A formal affair at which a tuxedo is required. However, the black suit option is also acceptable.

White Tie A highly formal affair requiring a tailcoat, white tie and white cummerbund or vest. Call for help.

Fashion & Personal Style: The Bottom Line

Personal style is not the same thing as fashion. Fashion is the latest offering from the garment industry. Your personal style is what makes you different from everyone else. It's about what looks good on you, how you combine things, what makes you feel comfortable and how you choose to portray yourself to the world around you.

All God's children are not beautiful....

...Most of God's children are, in fact, barely presentable. —Fran Lebowitz

7

Good Grooming

There was a time, not so long ago, when male vanity was seriously frowned upon. In the minds of many, it still is. However, the modern, metrosexual man knows something that the skeptics don't care to acknowledge. Taking care of yourself and taking pride in your appearance not only heightens your confidence, it makes you far more desirable in the sack.

Reasonable Vanity

Some may say that excessive vanity is indicative of a shallow nature and self-obsession. This is entirely true of *excessive* vanity. But a reasonable degree of vanity is simply indicative of self-respect and self-awareness. Tending to your appearance and feeling good about yourself does not mean you've lost the plot and chucked your integrity out the window. You may paint your house, but that doesn't mean the foundation is going to crumble. You'll just have a better-looking house.

With that little metaphor in mind, imagine the average woman being presented with two men from which to choose. Both men are of equal character, personality, integrity and masculinity. One has nice skin, good hair and clean feet, while the other one is dry, scaly and has nasty toenails. Well, you can see where this is headed. . . .

Hairstyles of the Rich and Famous

In the ever-changing world of hairstyles, maintaining the same look for too long can leave you looking laughably out of date. If you're still parting your hair on the side with a comb like you did in the third grade, or sporting a feathered do with a center part, it's time for you to get with the program. Drastic changes may not be necessary but a good hairstyle can add immeasurably to your appeal. This is not to suggest that you should frantically race after every trend and change your image constantly. On the contrary, it is far better to find a style that works for you, is easy to maintain and makes the best use of what you've got.

Obviously, the more hair you have, the greater your options, but that doesn't mean that every style will work for you. Before heading off to the hairstylist, flip through some magazines, see what your favorite movie star or sports star has going on, and find a style you think will work for you. Unless you're completely versed in the mysterious lingo of the hairstyling world, you'll do much better showing the stylist a photo rather than trying to explain what you envision. And even if the style you choose looks simple to you, there is probably more to the cut than you realize. That said, it's probably worth shelling out a few extra dollars to get a quality cut rather than getting another $7 hack-job. There is a big difference.

Primary Products

Once you've got the style you want, a variety of creams, balms, pomades and fudgelike substances are available to help sculpt and shape your creation, and you should ask your hairstylist which product is best for the look you're after. Remember that your favorite movie star's hair doesn't stand up like that on its own. Find out what you need to do.

Gel Best for thick or curly hair to sculpt, scrunch and shape into a wet look. Usually too heavy for fine or thinning hair. Avoid gels with alcohol that will dry the hair and may leave a flaky residue.

Mousse Yeah, it does have a bit of a clichéd '80s connotation, but a little dab still adds body and fullness to thin or fine hair. It can be used on wet hair for a sleek look or dry hair for a more natural look. For a natural look, just let it dry into the shape you want, then run your fingers through to break it up a bit.

Pomade A firm, fibrous substance used for shaping, texture and shine. Pomade is good for thick, short to medium haircuts to achieve spiky, tousled or messy looks, or for longer cuts, and can help you get that sexy, sleepy bed-head look. Apply a small amount by hand and stay away from the comb.

Sculpting lotion Good for short and chunky or naturally wavy styles. Adds firmness and lift without stiffness. Can be left as is for a wetter

There are an infinite number of hair products available for men.

look or broken up after drying for a more natural look. A good option for thinning hair to add a touch of shine and control.

Hairstyling sticks Similar in appearance to a deodorant stick, this waxy product is rubbed into the palms and fingers and then distributed through the hair. Best for choppy, spiky and slightly messy looks, and another option for bed-head chic.

Glossing wax A little dab can go a long way in adding shine and luster without locking hair into a set position. Hair retains its texture, but remains flexible and changeable.

In addition to those listed above, there are an infinite number of hair products available for men, so a little trial and error may be in order. And again, if you have no clue, just ask your hairstylist which product will work best for you.

Ten Tips for Better Hair

Unless you are a vampire or a magician, you should never try to dye your own hair. A little salt and pepper looks surprisingly distinguished on most men regardless of the length and style of your hair. Dying requires a lot of maintenance and is often far too easy to recognize. If you are just finding the odd gray hair here and there, you can always pluck the offenders as they appear, but when the process really gets going, it's sometimes best to hand over the reins to Mother Nature and let the new you emerge. That said, there's nothing wrong with adding a few stylish highlights, color treatments or dramatic color changes now and then. If professionally done, such treatments can make you look years younger. But home dye jobs meant to conceal your age usually backfire. Whatever the status of your coiffure, maintenance matters, so remember:

- "Lather, rinse and repeat" is a sales trick. One application will do.

- Alternate between two shampoos to keep hair responsive and healthy.
- Use protein shampoos to coat the hair shafts, add luster and increase fullness.
- For extremely dry hair, try leaving conditioner on for a half hour, then rinse.
- Blow dry, if you must, at the lowest setting to reduce damage to hair.
- Don't rely on the comb alone. The best hairstyles are achieved with a little finger action.
- Trim very short hairstyles every three or four weeks.
- Unless your hair is oily, skip a day of shampooing now and then, just use water.
- Work with what you've got. Don't try to disguise your curls or add unnatural waves to straight hair.
- If you need dandruff shampoo, get dandruff shampoo, but get conditioner too.

One application will do.

Is That Your Scalp I See?

For those with thinning hair, the rule of thumb is blissfully simple. Get over it and go short. You will not fool anyone by pouffing up what you have left to create some sort of sad illusion. It won't work. And, if you even consider a toupee, plugs or a comb-over, bear in mind that you will simply end up looking like a man with a toupee, plugs or a comb-over. There is infinitely more dignity in aging gracefully. If you keep your face and body in good shape, thinning hair should not diminish your sex appeal at all. In fact, in the eyes of many, it may even enhance it.

Happily, there are several lotions, pills and potions available to prevent and even reverse hair loss, and they're a perfectly valid option if you choose to go that route. Just do your research and don't waste your money on the magical cures.

Shaved.

Shaved with Tan

Comb-over.

FDA-approved topical solutions containing minoxidil, such as Rogaine (5%), and **DHT** inhibitors (in pill form), such as Propecia, are what you need and will require a prescription (2% minoxidil solutions are available over the counter). If you do choose to combat the cruelty of nature in this fashion, you should still keep your hair short in order to look good and more easily track your progress.

Whether you choose to go with the flow or chemically fend off Mother Nature, you should bear in mind that there are many international celebrities who have lost none of their popular or sexual appeal along with their hair. Andre Agassi, Michael Jordan and Bruce Willis all continue to exude vitality and magnetism while proudly displaying their genetic dispositions. Even stars with full heads of hair such as Matthew McConaughy, Justin Timberlake and David Beckham have been known to shave it all off in the name of fashion.

However, if you are among those who have a full head of hair and are considering a full buzz job, there are two important factors to consider. First, you need to have a well-shaped head. There is no point in shedding your mane if you're just going to end up revealing a pointed head or a myriad of bumps and dents. Second, and this is crucial, do not make the big move while you are sporting a tan. You'll end up looking like you're wearing a pink swim cap.

Skin Care

While many men place great importance on physical fitness and trendy hairstyles as ways of maintaining a youthful appearance, they completely ignore the one area where age is most evident—their skin. Ironically, there is no man who looks so haggard as the one with the huge, bulging muscles and the weathered, leathery face.

Because dehydrated skin ages more quickly, it is essential to drink lots of water. Keeping your skin clean is also vital as it allows perspiration to flow freely and toxins to be eliminated. For that reason, it's always a good idea to cleanse your face *before* working out as well as afterwards. This will allow your skin to cleanse itself naturally as you are perking up your pecs and aggravating your abs. As for your daily routine, a simple three-step process will keep your face looking its best:

- Cleanse your face with warm water (hot water dehydrates) and a glycerin-based soap rather than a harsher body bar.
- Use a gentle facial scrub in the shower to exfoliate and remove dead surface skin cells. You'd be surprised what's hanging on and lurking in those pores. It can also prevent ingrown hairs.
- Apply a quality facial moisturizer. Don't use that huge vat of body moisturizer—that's for your body. Find a good men's lotion that is formulated for the face and use it daily on your face and neck. Though moisturizers alone cannot reduce wrinkles, those containing antioxidants can help restore skin cells and help fend off new ones.

Additionally, you should get into the habit of applying a moisturizer to your body after showering. The skin on your arms, legs and torso is not immune to the aging process, so don't neglect it. You'll feel a lot better if you keep it supple and fresh, not only for yourself, but also for the person you've been getting close to.

Tanning

In recent decades, the depletion of the ozone layer along with a heightened awareness of skin cancer have taken much of the fun out of getting a nice tan. Still, it is undeniable that many of us simply look better with a little more color. Unfortunately, it is also undeniable that tanning can cause premature aging of the skin. In this arena, you'll have to make your own

Top Picks for Grooming Products
The top product lines favored by metrosexuals include Kiehl's, Clinique for Men and Aveda. Among the less pricey options, Nivea and Neutrogena also offer quality products, especially body moisturizers.

call as to whether or not it's worth the risk to get that golden glow the natural way. If you do choose to lie out in the sun, you should always use a sunblock with a minimum SPF of 15. If wrinkles are a concern, use SPF 30 on your face. The idea is to get a little extra color and glow, not to tan and burn to the point where you resemble a leather bag with eyes.

Of course, there are other methods by which you can bronze your epidermis. Tanning salons are an option, but you still need to use protective products. Most tanning salons will provide you with advice and several options in that area. But as of late, sunless tanning creams and lotions have become a far more popular alternative. Technology and cosmetology have improved greatly on those old potions that left unsuspecting subjects covered in orange streaks with little white patches in the spots they couldn't reach. Today, a variety of products are on the market that provide a far more natural, golden glow without streaking. If you're curious but reluctant, try out the product of your choice on your legs first. If it looks ridiculous, wear long pants until it fades and call it a day. If it looks good, do the rest of you, but remember to wash your hands. Nothing gives away the game like tanned palms.

Hands and Feet

Your hands and feet also require moisturizing. Your hands, in particular, are always on display so cleanliness and trimmed nails are essential. Presumably, fewer people are exposed to your feet, but those who are will certainly appreciate your efforts at maintenance. Again, in both business and romance, good grooming counts.

Manicures and pedicures are affordable luxuries that are indulged in regularly by rapidly increasing numbers of men. And though it may seem at first to be a laughable, fussy indulgence, most men who try it end up going back. Why? Because it feels great and it's hard to find anyone else who's willing to buff those nasty callouses off your toes and heels. If you do decide to splurge on either a manicure or pedicure, be sure to decline the offer of a clear polish. You don't want that.

Puff Daddy

One place where age and stress are most evident is the area around your eyes. If you're serious about looking good, there are several ways to treat this area where the skin is fine and delicate. Obviously, squinting contributes to wrinkles, so wearing sunglasses outdoors and eyeglasses when you need them will help. Washing your eyes with cold water will help keep them clear and supplementing your diet with vitamin A will help keep them bright.

There are also several eye creams on the market that will reduce fine lines and strengthen the skin. Apply them at night—who's gonna know? Puffiness can also be reduced by the application of a cold compress or various eye gels. But there is also a surprising home remedy for puffy eyes that is used by top supermodels and film stars, and it's blissfully inexpensive. Dabbing a little Preparation H cream (not gel) in the under-eye area will result in—no surprise here—shrinkage! Disregard any unpleasant associations and recognize that it's just a cream.

Carb Face
Consuming excessive amounts of carbohydrates can result in an unfortunate bloated appearance in the face not to mention the body. Beware.

Shaving & Facial Hair

Just as a woman's face can be recreated by variations in makeup, your look can be entirely transformed and reinvented by the way you deal with your facial hair. Goatees, closely trimmed beards and the length of your sideburns can define your face in ways that can work for or against you. Clean edges and lines can have a slimming effect on softer, rounded faces, and can also accentuate strong bone structure. Conversely, bushy moustaches or funky sideburns can leave you looking like a reject from the Village People.

The general rule for beardless sideburns is that they should end roughly at the bottom of your cheekbone. Longer sideburns go in and out of fashion and generally work best on slimmer faces with strong features. On rounder faces, they can drag everything down, creating an unfortunate, droopy look. Cut them too short and you'll end up with a disturbing Forrest Gump look. A very slight downward angle at the bottom of the sideburn can also add definition to your cheekbones.

Beards, goatees, soul patches and moustaches provide endless options, but should always be kept reasonably trimmed and cleanly edged. Even when going for a casually stubbled look, shaving beneath your jaw line is a subtle way to keep it looking clean and strong. Those with a thick, full beard have the greatest variety of options, but everyone can experiment a little on the weekend. Let your beard grow for a few days, and before shaving it all off, try something new. If it looks ridiculous, shave it off. If it's interesting, continue the experiment, let it come in a little more and see what kind of reaction you get.

Regardless of how you choose to sculpt your facial hair, there are some basic rules to getting the closest, cleanest shave possible:

- Shave *after* showering, when your pores are open and your skin is softer.
- If you have a heavy beard, a wet shave with a razor is always closer than an electric razor.
- Use warm water—hot water dehydrates the skin.
- Shaving cream is preferable to cheap foams containing alcohol, which often dry and irritate the skin.

- Allow the cream to soften your beard for a few minutes before shaving.
- Always use sharp blades. Discard disposable blades after four or five shaves.
- Shave in the direction of the hair growth if skin irritation or ingrown hairs are a problem.
- Avoid alcohol-based aftershaves. Use a toner or aftershave balm to close pores and tighten skin.

Eyebrows

Many men completely underestimate the importance of eyebrows when considering their appearance. The thought of plucking and tweezing leaves them squirming in discomfort for fear that they will end up looking like a drag queen on an off day. But the truth is, that a little cleaning up around the edges can make a huge difference. Nearly every time you see a comedian parodying a politician or anchorman on television, they are sporting huge, fake eyebrows that instantly define the character and draw huge laughs on their own. Keep that in mind.

The first step in taming your hedges is to invest in a good pair of tweezers. Don't even think about shaving around the edges or you will surely regret it. It's best to tackle the problem after a hot shower, when your pores are open. You can start by removing any long, wiry, renegade hairs that look as though they might be picking up radio signals. Nobody wants to look at those. Just get hold of them and pluck them in the direction of your ears to minimize the discomfort.

Once you have recovered from the anxiety of your first pass, zero in on those hairs beneath the arch of the brow that are standing alone. Do not get carried away and don't drift into the main lawn or you'll be drifting into dangerous territory. You also want to get those hairs growing too far down the sides of your eyes. Those are the ones that cause your eyes to look droopy and tired. Your goal should be a natural, clean look with a generally even line.

Unless you enjoy frightening small children, you'll also need to tackle the area in between the brows. The clean space between your brows should be about the width of your finger. Just remove the hairs in that space without creating an abrupt, unnatural line at the inner edges of the brows. If you are at all reluctant about any of these steps, it might be wise to go to a professional the first time around, and then you can just maintain what they started.

Nose and Ears

Time to Unplug?

If you have blackheads on your nose, a little trip to the pharmacy is in order. Biore nose strips are a quick and effective way to remedy the situation. Follow the instructions carefully and be amazed.

One of Mother Nature's cruelest tricks is that as men age, and their foreheads grow taller and their ankles go bald, all that hair seems not to disappear, but rather it reemerges from the nostrils and ears. Though there is scant scientific evidence to support this theory, most men over thirty will attest to the strange phenomenon.

In any case, this is an area of male grooming that no man can afford to ignore. There is nothing more repulsive than long hairs hanging out of your nose. You may not be able to see them, but the person staring you in the face can see little else. For about ten dollars you can buy electric nose-and-ear hair clippers in any pharmacy and be rid of the problem. The slight tickling sensation you'll experience is far better than the pain of plucking in this case.

Ear hairs figure somewhat less prominently in the grand scheme, but are still an unpleasant surprise when detected. They can emerge not only from the ear canal, but also along the rim of the ear, where they cleverly evade your notice. Remember, the rest of the world sees you from all sides, so you must be ever-vigilant as these wiry devils can crop up quite suddenly. Lean into the mirror, look closely and pluck all offenders on a regular basis.

Body Hair

The amount of body hair you have is a matter of genetics. Luckily, sexual attraction is such that there are some who prefer a man's body to be smooth, while others find a degree of hairiness to be very masculine and sexy. Most men fall in the middle somewhere. For total hair removal, several professional treatments are available, including waxing, electrolysis and laser hair removal. For major transformations, a little research and expense can provide happy results. However, waxing is temporary and both electrolysis and laser hair removal usually require repeat treatments before lasting results can be achieved.

If the fuss and expense of professional treatments don't interest you, you can always try a depilatory cream or home waxing kits. Creams require nothing more than a single application, a waiting period and a shower, while waxing can be a bit painful and difficult in hard-to-reach areas. Still, both are valid options you can try in the privacy of your home.

A pair of electric clippers with varying comb sizes is a cheap investment that can improve the appearance of your body drastically. Shaving in areas with sparse hair is acceptable, but shaving a very hairy area will only result in stubble and discomfort. Unless you are determined to be completely hairless, it is best to simply keep what you've got under relative control.

Arms and legs are often best left alone, but trimming your chest, stomach and underarm hair can enhance a well-defined body. This is often evidenced in the advertisement of home exercise equipment on television, where the "before" photo is often chubby and hairy while the "after" photo is muscular and miraculously hairless. Anything less than a half inch may look unnatural, but it is entirely up to you. Experiment a little to see what looks best on you. Just remember, it never looks right to have body hairs peering over your shirt collar.

Your Naughty Bits

At this point we come to a most delicate subject, in more ways than one. In this age of sexual liberation, the sophisticated man may at any given time find himself involved in a variety of shameless explorations, gymnastic gyrations and welcome violations. That being the case, it is wise to keep oneself in good form from head to toe.

Now, just as you wouldn't want a romantic prospect to wander into your bedroom without having a chance to tidy up, it is most unwise to allow a lover to journey to your nether regions without the same consideration. As always, a little house cleaning goes a long way. Use the clippers, make sure you're sober and don't get carried away.

Needless to say, cleanliness is paramount. In addition to a little pruning and trimming, the sensible man will also engage in a little moisturizing and, when feeling especially frisky, a nice, fresh scent makes for a pleasant surprise. It should be noted, however, that this last step should always be administered with a light touch. Anything more may result in sneezing, suspicion and other unpleasantness.

Scents and Sensibility

Unfortunately, many men are completely unaware of their own body odors. While there is no need to be paranoid, it is important to recognize that at any moment in time you may be emitting more than charm. For that reason, every man should be aware of the preventative measures that can help keep problems from developing in the first place.

- Professional teeth cleaning every six months will do wonders for your breath.
- Mouthwash is a temporary fix, but gargling with hydrogen peroxide and water can help gum disease.
- When dining out, eating a sprig of parsley or a lemon rind can help mask nasty breath caused by garlic or onions.
- Keep breath mints in your desk drawer at work for a quick fix before meetings.
- Use deodorant soap rather than regular soap to kill odor-causing bacteria.
- Scrub your skin thoroughly in the shower with scrubbing gloves or a loofah sponge.
- Chlorophyll tablets taken with meals can act as a natural internal deodorizer.
- Wear cotton socks that breathe rather than synthetic ones.
- Change your shoes daily to allow them to dry out.

The Creep Checklist

Your personal preferences in regard to grooming are your own. You may decide to go for a complete overhaul, or you may decide that you are perfectly happy with your big, bad, rugged self. Feeling comfortable and happy with your appearance is what matters most. However, there are certain revolting oversights that will universally result in horrified looks and potential lovers fleeing for the nearest exit. You must never allow yourself, under any circumstances, to be caught exhibiting any of the following traits:

- Abnormal body odor
- Protruding nose hairs
- Crazy ear hairs
- Free-standing mystery hairs
- Toupees or comb-overs

- Farmer/trucker tans
- Dirty fingernails
- Bad breath
- Crusty toes
- A mullet

Good Grooming: The Bottom Line

You may polish and wax the car, but it's still the engine that matters the most. Good grooming counts for a lot, but if you find yourself in a panic because you've misplaced your Kiehl's lotion, you may want to sit down and reflect a bit.

Don't stay in bed,...

...unless you can make money in bed. —George Burns

8

Body & Fitness

In the realms of fashion, automobiles and investment strategies, the modern ideal is an ever-changing proposition. So it is with body types. Without a doubt, the ideal body image for the new, twenty-first-century, metrosexual man is natural, lean and trim. The pumped-up, steroid-injecting muscleman is out, and a healthier, slim physique is now in.

Thankfully, this new silhouette stops short of the unhealthy, waifish extreme that has been thrust upon women for several decades now. The new man may be lean, but he is also toned and muscular. Shoulders, chests, arms, legs and abs are still defined, but not to cartoonish proportions.

The Metrosexual Ideal

The good news here is that you no longer need to spend countless hours in the gym straining and groaning to achieve unnaturally bulbous muscles. The bad news is that you may have to cut back a bit on the pasta and pizza. Though losing those few extra pounds may be a drag, it is undeniable that lower body fat equals greater energy and a healthier heart. It seems there is a newfound respect for Mother Nature's original design as well as the FDA's suggested height-to-body-weight ratio.

Of course, different men have different genetic predispositions, and a little dieting and exercise won't turn the average man into a six-foot, one-hundred-and-seventy-five-pound Adonis. However, it is encouraging to know that your own ideal is simply the healthiest, trimmest version of what you've already got. Granted, a little extra effort may be required to enhance a few key areas, but the old image of the skinny guy getting sand kicked in his face by the muscle-bound bully is history.

Evidence of the new slimmer ideal can be seen in the shifting focus of men's fashions. Looser, boxier styles are being rejected in favor of narrower cuts, fitted shirts and slim-line jackets. And though this may seem new, fashion trends always go in cycles, and we have seen this before. It's all a variation on the styles of the early- to mid-1960s when JFK, the Rat Pack, James Bond and the Beatles were all sporting narrow trousers and slim-cut suits. And if those men seemed to be able to keep it together in their day without too much trouble, there's no reason you can't do the same and slip into a trimmer silhouette.

The Muscle Guy If you did overdo it a bit in the '90s and now find yourself peering over your enormous pectorals at these pages, you may want to think about slimming down slightly. Enjoy the opportunity to ease up and let those muscles shrink back a bit to more reasonable proportions. You can still maintain the strength and tone you have worked so hard to achieve, but your new, more modest proportions will make you look far better both in and out of your clothes.

- Continue your workout regimen, but lower the weights to maintain tone without increasing size.
- Lower your caloric intake as you will be burning less energy.
- Spend more time on cardiovascular exercise and less on weight training.

The Skinny Guy If you're naturally skinny, you're in luck. You've got the right body type to pull off the latest looks that are headed your way. However, being a good clothes hanger may not be enough. Every man needs a little bit of shape and that may require some effort if you aren't naturally blessed with a classic, V-shaped torso. Additionally, while many naturally thin men have a flat stomach and good abs, many others do not. It is entirely possible to be thin and still be flabby, especially in the midsection. The idea is to be toned all over, so don't think you're off the hook because your soft parts are cleverly disguised.

- Invest in a pair of dumbbells to add some shape and tone to your shoulders, chest and arms. Regular flys, presses and curls can produce quick results and give your torso some proportion.

Your Body Type
Obviously, you need to work with what you've got, and while some will want to slim down, others may need to bulk up a tad here and there. In any case, a few simple adjustments will help get you on track to the perfect version of yourself.

- Squats and lunges may be in order to prevent chicken-leg syndrome. They'll also help create butts for the buttless.
- Eating extra protein will help build muscle more quickly.

The Heavy Guy Well, you know where you need to begin. Cutting back on carbohydrates and increasing your intake of protein is an obvious starting point, but any formal diet will depend on your health and you should consult your doctor for his or her recommendation for maximum results. However, you don't have to wait until you're skinny before you start to tone up. You can begin strengthening the muscles beneath the extra pounds while you're losing the weight. Do both at the same time and you'll reach your goals twice as fast.

- Fat-burning, cardiovascular exercise is the key for you, but you should find something you enjoy doing to make it less of a chore. It could be walking, jogging, aerobics or any sport that gets you moving.
- Drink a lot of water. It will help flush out toxins and will keep you feeling full, so you're less likely to snack and cheat.
- Incorporate the sauna or the steam room into your workout regimen, and let those sweat glands do their thing. (And don't forget to take a bottle of water with you.)

Spee-do, Spee-don't
In the final poolside analysis, modesty prevails as shorts are still preferable to the basket-hugging Speedo. However, freedom reigns on private yachts and in your own backyard.

The Three Most Important Areas

Regardless of your body type, there are three key areas that matter most in the sexual appeal of the male physique. This is not to imply that the whole package isn't the most important thing, but as you zero in on your target weight, pay close attention to the following areas and you'll be doing yourself a huge favor:

Chest and shoulders Massive muscles are not the goal, but some nice definition and a little shape will make you look infinitely better in shirts and jackets and will give you more confidence when the shirt comes off.

Stomach A six-pack isn't necessary, but a flat stomach is ideal. A small waist will make your upper body look better and will make all your clothes, and especially your pants, hang better on you.

Butt There's no denying it. Everybody notices the butt. If you can get that caboose in shape, you will get a lot of attention and you will be handsomely rewarded.

Daily Workouts

If you are a die-hard gym rat, chances are you've already got your training program in place and the idea of working out at home may not be of interest to you. But if you're not a fan of the gym, or if you travel a lot and spend a great deal of time in hotel rooms, a regular routine of exercise is relatively easy to incorporate into your day. While exercising in the morning can give you a nice energy boost to start your day, it also involves waking up earlier, and for some that just may be too much to ask. But morning or evening, a little effort goes a long way, and there's no need to invest in weird contraptions or space-skiing machines.

Depending on your enthusiasm and your desire for speedy results, you should plan on incorporating some or all of the following exercise into your daily routine at least three to five times a week. The number of repetitions is up to you, but the key is to do three full sets of each exercise. Simply doing the minimum will increase your strength and flexibility even if you don't see immediate visible results. And as far as your level of enthusiasm is concerned, try not to get carried away.

3
Preferred Sportswear Lines
....,,

Adidas

Puma

Nike

Overdo it and you'll find yourself at the office the next day unable to lift a paper cup of coffee.

You can buy all the fitness magazines you want, but invariably the "new workouts," "easy exercises" and "miracle programs" all boil down to the same elements in the end. The exercises may be old-school, but they're still the safest, easiest and most effective:

Crunch sit-ups Simple crunches with knees bent, hands behind the head and elbows wide are still the most effective way to work your abs. Add a twisting motion to work the sides.

Push-ups The perfect exercise to work the arms, chest and shoulders to provide even, natural-looking results. Keep your back straight and hands shoulder width apart. To isolate different muscle groups, try placing your hands wider apart or closer together.

Lunges A quick and easy way to firm up those all-important glutes. Stand up straight, step one foot forward, gently lower your back knee to the floor, then return to standing position. Alternate legs and repeat until you feel it.

Dumbbells Invest in a pair (the weight depends on your strength—don't be too ambitious) and do sets of flys and sets of presses while lying on your back. In a seated position, rest your elbow on your knee for curls, and sit straight up for overhead presses. Do repeated sets of each exercise, one at a time.

Stretching An essential part of strengthening that will increase circulation and flexibility. Sit on the floor with a straight back and legs extended parallel. Reach for your ankles and hold for thirty seconds. Relax and repeat three times. As your flexibility increases over time, the goal should be to eventually rest your head on your knees with a straight back. Ha! Do the same in a straddle position. Reach for one ankle and hold for thirty seconds, then the other ankle, then reach forward in the middle. Relax and repeat three times.

A Worthy Challenge

Try to master the handstand. Start by using a wall to back you up, then keep practicing until you can stand freely on your own for 60 seconds. Master that and you've got a new party trick.

Try to master the handstand.

Sports and the City

For the urban metrosexual, sports and athletic activities are no less important than they are to his country cousins. And, luckily, most cities have an abundance of sporting facilities for every inclination. Whether you lean toward the extreme or the genteel, regular sporting activity is an integral part of life for the modern man.

You already know which sports you like, and if you can join a league or hook up regularly with friends, you'll be doing yourself a huge favor on many levels. You'll be getting fit while having fun, you'll increase your social circle and you'll be shedding stress on a consistent basis. Your choice of sport may be dictated by time or finances, but there are plenty of options to choose from and it never hurts to try something new every now and then.

Extreme Sports

For those who crave an adrenaline rush, extreme sports can offer a tremendous high. For others the idea of jumping off a bridge tethered only to an elastic cord is about as appealing as, well . . . jumping off a bridge attached to an elastic cord. In any case it's your call whether you want to try any of the following activities:

Bungee jumping Your mind knows you're bungee jumping, but your nervous system will think you've jumped out a window. Dignity Factor: Medium

Skydiving The classic adventure for adrenaline junkies always makes for good cocktail party conversation. Dignity Factor: High

Heli-skiing Mountaintop drop-offs for extreme skiers who consider ski lifts and black diamond runs amateur business. Dignity Factor: High

Snowboarding An endless variety of half-pipe rollovers, aerial somersaults and major wipeouts provide mega-thrills for adventurous snow surfers. Dignity Factor: Medium

Hang gliding A peaceful, serene extreme, unless of course you're terrified of heights. Dignity Factor: Medium

Mountain climbing Man vs. mountain on precipitous ridgelines or ice-capped peaks. A supreme test of endurance, courage and tenacity. Dignity Factor: High

Whitewater rafting An exciting and exhilarating adventure to be shared with friends, lovers and other strangers. Dignity Factor: Medium

Street luge A curious endeavor for the young at heart and the desperately bored—careening down a paved course on your back on a metal cart. Dignity Factor: Low

Zorbing Out of ideas? How about bouncing down a hillside inside a huge, inflatable plastic ball? Dignity Factor: Low

Money Sports, Rentals and Inexpensive Ideas

Certain sports such as skiing, golf and tennis often involve private clubs or exclusive resorts not always accessible to the average guy. Then again, there are ski rentals, public tennis courts and public golf courses, so there's really nothing to prevent you from enjoying any sport you may choose. Well, maybe polo, but there are still plenty of activities in which you can participate that require little or no expense at all.

Check the following list to see if there's something out there that you haven't tried, or something that you'd like to pursue either at home or while on vacation:

- Skiing
- Tennis
- Golf
- Jet-skiing
- Parasailing
- Kayaking
- Biking
- Rock climbing
- Scuba diving
- Boogie boarding
- Hiking
- Rollerblading
- Jogging
- Swimming
- Yoga
- Basketball
- Beach volleyball
- Sex

**Sporting Events
Most Likely to Appeal
to the Metrosexual**
NBA basketball games
World Cup soccer matches
WTA Tennis tournaments
Olympic events
World Cup skiing

**Sporting Events
Least Likely to Appeal
to the Metrosexual**
Professional wrestling
Swimnastics
Rodeo
Tractor pulls
Figure skating

The Inner Workout

The flip side of the rigorous sporting life is the development of one's internal self and the ability to truly, deeply and completely relax. Spirituality, inner peace—call it what you will—

but in today's chaotic and frenzied world, it's worth looking into. The desired state of inner calm and decompression can be achieved in more ways than one:

Yoga & Pilates Physical training in both yoga and pilates has grown tremendously in popularity in recent years. Both offer a variety of benefits, including a reduced heart rate, greater flexibility and increased strength. While pilates is similar to resistance training with an emphasis on stretching, the more strenuous forms of yoga, such as Hatha, can provide a surprisingly thorough workout. Both are worth investigating as ideal ways to work out without bulking up.

Martial Arts A number of martial arts, from karate to Tae Kwon Do, combine strength, power, mental focus and a state of inner calm into a single discipline. The exploration of mind over matter along with strength training and the development of self-defense skills have made martial arts training increasingly popular among young, urban men.

Spa Treatments By far, the easiest and most luxurious route to take to achieve inner peace is a nice long visit to the spa. The supremely relaxing effects of being pampered from head to toe have made the spa experience the new church of the modern, metrosexual man. The sheer pleasure is matched only by the very real physical benefits of massage, skin treatments, eucalyptus steam rooms and full-body scrubs. Fair warning to the uninitiated: It's all very addictive.

Massage Options

Beyond the obvious pleasures of human contact and muscle relaxation, massage offers a variety of health benefits, including reduced stress and anxiety, increased circulation, calming of the nervous system and energy restoration. Sure, it's an indulgence, but as indulgences go, it's a worthwhile investment in your own well-being. Here again you have options:

Swedish The Western approach involving long, deep strokes with light oils applied to the body. Intended to relax soft tissues and muscles, energize the body and stimulate circulation. Supremely indulgent.

Shiatsu A far more aggressive approach incorporating deep tissue manipulation and intense acupressure intended to balance the flow of yin and yang. Free your Chi!

Deep tissue Focused on the connection and interaction of the muscles and connective tissues of the body. Pressure points and deep muscle massage release both muscular and emotional tension. Not for the squeamish.

Sports massage Vigorous, deep manipulation of isolated muscles and joints to prevent and/or treat sports injuries. More functional than indulgent.

Reiki A more mystical, healing approach utilizing a light touch and visualization to maximize energy flow, align chakras and stimulate internal organs. Belief equals relief.

Reflexology Based on the premise that the application of pressure to specific areas of the body can stimulate the internal organs to which they are connected. Often focused on the feet. Not for the ticklish.

Sensual massage with a happy ending Usually a house call. You figure it out.

Body & Fitness: The Bottom Line

The enlightened metrosexual knows that a healthy body is complemented by internal and mental vitality. Attending to the combination of the two dimensions can result in increased energy, clarity of mind and heightened sexual awareness.

There is hardly anyone whose sexual life,
if it were broadcast,...

...would not fill the world at large with surprise and horror. —W. Somerset Maugham

9

Sex & Romance

One of the defining characteristics of the metro-sexual man is that he is beyond sexual stereotypes. He knows who he is and what he wants. For that very reason, he feels no compulsion to defend his masculinity through posturing or threatening others. The metrosexual man knows that in order to be comfortable with himself, he needs to allow others to be themselves. The heterosexuality, bisexuality, or homosexuality of anyone else does not concern him, unless of course he is romantically interested in that person. Then he needs to know.

Diversity

Thankfully, life is not a black and white proposition. Most of us live and operate in the gray areas. People are inevitably far more complex than they might first appear to be, and to go through life trying to pigeonhole others is both exhausting and futile. You never know. It's pointless to label others and you shouldn't worry about who's labeling you. Just live your life and appreciate the diversity of those around you. The metrosexual man enjoys positive attention and feels free to flirt with both women and men in a light-hearted, fun manner. Flirting is harmless and flattery is just that—flattery. So, lighten up, have fun and be who you want to be. If you're going to make the effort to look your best, you shouldn't freak out when people respond positively.

Dating

If there is any one area where all of your personal habits and behavioral practices come into play, it is in the realm of dating. The delicate dance that is performed as two people feel each other out (and possibly up) in search of compatibility can be great fun or entirely excruciating. When anxiety, insecurity and social blunders enter the picture, things can go downhill in a hurry and an evening can stretch into eternity.

If you have decided that you want to meet someone, you need to take action. The best way to start is to make eye contact and see if you can elicit a smile. If there is interest, more looks should be forthcoming and the game may be under way. Once you've decided to approach, enter into the situation with some light flirtation and casual conversation. It is during this initial period of socializing that you can determine whether or not there is a mutual attraction to begin with. If for any reason the response is lukewarm, you can always make a graceful getaway without having humiliated yourself.

While the exchange of phone numbers is a promising sign, it does not necessarily guarantee that a date will follow. Second thoughts, nasty hangovers or any number of unforeseen complications may derail the process, so if you make the call and get an answering service, just leave a message and wait to hear back. You may try a second call, but you don't want to be the guy who keeps calling over and over, explaining what he meant by his last message and wondering if somehow his messages are being accidentally erased. They're not.

Once a date has been made, you'll want to present yourself at your best. Chances are, the best you is the one who is happy, relaxed and comfortable. Of course, you should look your best, but you don't want to show up with a suspicious tan or a frighteningly shellacked new hairdo. Any attempt to be someone you are not will ultimately backfire, so don't set yourself up.

A first date is sure to be uncomfortable if either of the parties involved feel that they are being evaluated, or that they are auditioning for the other. Don't put yourself in that position, and don't subject your date to that kind of uncomfortable scrutiny either. Try to relax and have fun as if you're hanging out with a new friend, which ideally you are. Just concentrate on the activity that you've arranged and let the conversation flow naturally. Here are a few additional dos and don'ts to keep in mind while you're on your date.

Dating Dos and Don'ts

Do maintain eye contact and remember to smile from time to time. You're there to get to know one another, not hide from one another.
Don't stare at the floor and look morose. It's understandable to be nervous, but don't let it paralyze you.

Do ask questions and remember to listen. Show some interest in finding out more about your date.

Don't hog the conversation and bring everything back to you. You want to share the spotlight.

Do keep your conversation positive and maintain a pleasant demeanor. **Don't** whine, complain or ramble on about your personal problems, your evil boss or your unbearable family.

Do allow for occasional silences. Sometimes it's very nice to sit quietly together.
Don't fill every second with nervous chatter, and don't divulge all your secrets, problems and hang-ups.

Do keep an open mind and give your date the benefit of the doubt.
Don't be judgmental and look for flaws. Everyone has them, and so do you.

Do give your date your full attention and focus on making her comfortable.
Don't accept calls on your cell phone or stare at others.

Do stay in the moment and allow intimacy and physical contact to develop naturally.
Don't obsess over how it's going or whether you're going to have sex later.

Do be polite and considerate throughout the date, even if it isn't going well.
Don't say you'll call again if you don't mean it, and don't worry if it doesn't work out.

Do pay attention to sexual signals and be open to whatever develops.
Don't come on too strong or push for sex too soon. You might ruin a really great beginning.

Ten Alternative Ideas for Dates

If the idea of sitting across a dinner table from a relative stranger fills you with dread—imagining forced conversation and extended silences—

Do pay attention to sexual signals and be open to whatever develops.

Don't come on to strong or push for sex too soon. You might ruin a really great beginning.

there are a number of other options available for that first date. Choosing a more lively activity will provide diversion, lighten the pressure and help avoid that awkward feeling of sitting through a job interview. Consider one or more of these options:

- Go for a long walk along a beach, pier or riverwalk.
- Check out a museum exhibition.
- Go for an afternoon hike.
- Get tickets to an outdoor concert in the park.
- Take a boat ride.
- Visit a planetarium.
- See a revival of a film classic.
- Take a day trip to a winery.
- Choose a funky cabaret or jazz bar.
- Go to a street fair, festival or cheesy amusement park.

A Note on Chivalry

Despite the grumblings of disgruntled modernists, chivalry is not yet dead. However, different women respond to gentlemanly behavior in different ways depending on the setting. While business situations require a balance of good manners and professional respect, romantic situations usually are more appropriate for a touch of the gallant. Though some may find chivalrous behavior unnecessary, most women will appreciate the effort as long as you are subtle and don't make a big production of it. A gentleman will always:

- Walk nearest the street on a sidewalk.
- Help a woman on and off with her coat.
- Follow her to a table in a restaurant, but precede her through a crowd.
- Offer her his arm when entering or departing from a social function.
- Open doors and pull out chairs.
- Allow the woman to order first.
- Rise slightly whenever a woman arrives at or leaves from a table.
- Escort a woman all the way home.

- Pick up any item she may drop along the way.
- Pay.

    The key is to be subtle and natural. No woman will appreciate you lunging in front of her as she reaches for a door, or forcing her aside so you can be nearest to the curb.

Seduction

At its best, seduction is truly an art form. It can take place in a single evening or over a long period of time. It is a sensual process that can be extremely erotic and even intoxicating for both the seducer and the person being seduced. It is a psychological process that builds anticipation, heightens arousal and almost always results in better sex.

    Once you've made the decision that you'd like to have sex, you need to set an appropriate tone and follow through. Timidity and hesitation do not usually yield exciting results, but neither does a clumsy and aggressive approach. A slow seduction can be a great deal of fun and as exciting as the actual sex that is likely to follow. Try these simple steps to build anticipation:

- A little, subtle innuendo in an e-mail or over the phone can communicate your interest.
- Plan ahead by creating the right mood with music, candles and lighting.
- Make time for wine and conversation.
- When in public, a soft light touch is far more erotic than clinging to your date.
- In private, focus your attentions on different parts of your lover's body.
- Pay close attention to the hands, the feet, the neck, the ears, the shoulders and the scalp.
- Incorporate a slow, deep massage into the proceedings.

5

Things Best Done Naked

....

Sex

Sleeping

Swimming

Stretching

Phone calls

The thing to remember is that you can extend the erotic experience by pacing it slowly. There is no need to rush toward the finish line, and by focusing on your partner's pleasure, you will not only benefit from reciprocal pleasures, but you will also be remembered as a truly great lover.

Your Sexual Self

In today's society there is a virtual panoply of sexual possibilities available to the modern metrosexual man. Regardless of your persuasion, your preferences or your favorite position, there is someone out there for you, and once you have lured that someone into your innermost orbit, you want to make sure they find it's a nice place to be. This does not mean that you need to perform handsprings or swing from the chandelier to impress. It does mean that you need to be confident and aware of what you are doing.

In order to feel confident in the bedroom, you need to start by working on yourself. While working out may get your body in shape, it is more important to get your mind in shape. You can start by taking a serious look at your inhibitions, and then addressing each of them individually. Whatever your insecurities—and every man has them—the only way to get over them is to face each one down and decide what you can do to bring about change.

What is undermining your confidence and keeping you from extending yourself and enjoying a healthy sex life? Is it your weight? If so, a firm resolve to get in shape may be enough to turn things around. If your weight is a symptom of some deeper issues, you need to be honest with yourself and consider how you can address those issues. Then again, you may decide that you're just being too hard on yourself. Not everyone is attracted to skinny, hairless man-boys, so embrace who you are and recognize that what you *do* in the bedroom is

5

Things Not to Do Naked

....

Carpentry

Paperwork

Building a fire

Cooking bacon

Anything involving Krazy Glue

far more important than how you look splayed across the sheets.

Residual psychological issues such as sexual shame or guilt may require some serious introspection on your part or they may require professional help. In any case, acknowledging the problem is the first step, and if you can get into the habit of encouraging yourself and reminding yourself that sex should be a healthy and happy experience, you will at least be headed in the right direction. However, issues such as these are usually deeply rooted so don't expect them to disappear on their own.

Lack of experience is a temporary situation and premature ejaculation can sometimes be corrected by concentrating on sensation and breathing. A little experimentation on your own can familiarize you with the contractions you experience before going over the edge, and by controlling your pace and pulling back you may be able to increase your stamina. If not, a short discussion with your doctor may be in order. Don't be embarrassed, he's a doctor—he won't care.

The Long and Short of It

Of course, the most common source of sexual anxiety among men is penis size. Most studies indicate that the average size of a grown man's erect penis is between five and six inches. However, penile length is hardly the only measure of how satisfying a lover you can be. While you may be obsessed with your own member, chances are your lover is taking the whole package into consideration. What you do and how you make your partner feel is a huge factor in determining your desirability as a lover. In fact, being on the larger end of the scale can often present greater problems of discomfort and awkwardness. So relax and take the focus off of yourself by concentrating on your partner's pleasure.

Another thing to remember is that most sexual relationships will benefit from a little variety over time. While each relationship will progress at its own pace, you may want to consider the following:

- Learn from your partner's responses, and let them guide you. Also pay attention to your own responses. You may be surprised.
- Remain open to undiscovered areas of your own body that enjoy a bit of attention. There is no part of your anatomy that you should be panicky or self-conscious about. Let your lover know what you like and don't like.
- Pillows, chairs and carpeted stairs can spice things up, though tables must always be tested in advance to avoid unexpected trips to the hospital.
- Blankets are always a sensible idea for sex in the great outdoors.
- A trip to the sex shop together can be a fun way to introduce a few toys.
- Even the diminutive Dr. Ruth encourages fantasy, so communicate and find out what your partner might be open to.
- Role-playing can be fun if both of you are up for the game.
- Uniforms and situations involving authority figures can be fun, though it's probably not advisable to show up unexpectedly on your lover's doorstep dressed as a Nazi.

The most important thing is to find out what both of you enjoy and are comfortable with. Sex does not have to be complicated or theatrical to be good. It simply depends on the two (or more?) people involved and their personal tastes.

Sexual Dos and Don'ts

Do make an effort to be creative and exciting in bed.

Don't try to imitate what you've seen in porno films. Those are bad actors having bad sex.

Do use your mouth and your breath in an erotic way.
Don't just thrust your tongue out. Use it creatively or put it away.

Do experiment slowly with degrees of pressure.
Don't bite, unless requested.

Do mix things up a bit.
Don't keep repeating the same action over and over.

Do speak to your lover and ask what they like.
Don't assume dirty talk is welcome. Feel it out gradually.

Do make eye contact and be aware of your own facial expressions.
Don't scrunch up your face and stare at the wall.

Do remember that the entire body can become erotically charged.
Don't just go for the obvious spots.

Do allow yourself to enjoy
the emotional connection.

Do allow yourself to be aggressive and dominant.
Don't ever allow yourself to become bullying or insensitive.

Do maintain affection and sensitivity as things wind down.
Don't roll over and go to sleep after you climax.

Do allow yourself to enjoy the emotional connection.
Don't cry afterwards.

Don't cry afterwards.

A Word About Safe Sex

The metrosexual man is safe, he's healthy and he is never careless. Obviously, you should never do anything that you are uncomfortable with, and certainly avoid anything that is unsafe. Condoms should always be used in the beginning of any relationship, and should be used with caution. Air pockets in a condom can lead to breakage, so it is important to squeeze the air from the tip before rolling the condom down. Oil-based lubricants can degrade latex, so be sure you are using a water-based lubricant. Additionally, you may want to experiment with different condom sizes on your own to ensure comfort and convenience.

As for safe-sex guidelines, you are an adult, and it is your responsibility to educate yourself. Don't rely on what others tell you—find out for yourself by reading up on safe-sex guidelines or talking to your doctor. Sexually transmitted diseases are serious business and to engage in sexual activity without knowing the facts is the height of stupidity.

Sex & Romance: The Bottom Line

Being a great lover means taking the focus off of yourself. In the realm of the boudoir, you tend to get what you give, so don't be selfish. Though your sex life may have started out as a solo endeavor, there is now another person there with you, so enjoy yourself, be free and appreciate the fact that you've found a friend to share the fun.

Never keep up with the Joneses....

...Drag them down to your level. —Quentin Crisp

10

Home Décor

So, you've got the right clothes, some good music and you're confident about your personal grooming? That's all very well, but the picture is not yet complete. Your home is also a reflection of your personal style and has a great psychological effect on how you feel about yourself and your world. Waking up every morning in a cluttered, messy, and ugly space is not going to start you off in a happy and confident mood. At the end of the day you want to be able to return to comfortable and pleasant surroundings, especially if you are not returning home alone.

Disguising Your Lack of Taste

It isn't necessary to spend buckets of money to improve your living space. A lot can be accomplished by rearranging what you've already got. Begin by clearing out everything that you do not need. Throw away or donate everything that is old, outdated or neglected. If you can't bear to part with sentimental stuff, box it and store it. If you want to make a little extra cash, call up a friend and have a yard sale or log onto Ebay.

Once the useless stuff has been removed, you can slowly improve your surroundings by upgrading your everyday appliances and functional items. Begin by replacing that old shower curtain, that '70s alarm clock, the grungy trash can and that phone with the crazy, twisted cord. Take a look around you and see what's really got to go, and then make the changes over time as your budget allows. Once you get started, the ball will have begun rolling and the transformation will have begun.

Furnishings

The furnishings you choose for your home are the basic building blocks of home design. For this reason, as you begin to upgrade you living space, you need to be sure that the furniture makes sense as a whole. The first step is to decide on a general theme and make sure all the pieces adhere to that theme. Mixing elements is not a problem, but you don't want to completely lose the plot.

In order for things to hang together properly, you need to have recurring elements. A good starting point is the wood, if in fact there is any. Is it consistent throughout the room? Dark woods create a warmer, heavier feeling that works well with Indian, Latin or African art, or for a sophisticated English library look. Lighter, blonde woods are best for a more modern, Scandinavian feeling that goes well with brighter colors or cool blues and grays for a calm, clean look. Rough, weathered woods can be used for a rustic, country effect. When mixed with antiques and thrift store finds, mismatched pieces can create an eclectic and comfortable space. Combining antiques with contemporary pieces is fine as long as there are some common or complementary elements involved.

A quick trip to the hardware store for some sandpaper, brushes and wood stain or paint is all it takes to turn around a bad situation. Just don't make the mistake of trying to stain any wood surfaces that have been shellacked or treated without sanding first. You'll be in the retirement home before the stain seeps through to the wood.

As for upholstery, your couch and chairs should be complementary, but not necessarily the same. Though you can find living room sets of good quality, it is far better to combine individual pieces to add unique character to a room and avoid that boxed-set look. Quality leather is always a strong—though usually expensive—choice, and where fabrics are concerned you should probably avoid stripes, plaids and floral prints unless you really know what you're doing. Go for solids and let some colorful cushions do the talking.

Your options in regard to rugs and floor coverings depend on what you have to begin with. Wood floors provide the greatest opportunity to define spaces and add character with area rugs. From modern to Moroccan, your choice should reflect the general motif of your furnishings. Wall-to-wall carpeting is often best left uncluttered and unobstructed if it is quality carpeting. However, if you are renting a space with bland, low-pile carpeting, a nice area rug can be a very effective improvement. If by some cruel twist of fate you inherit a space with wall-to-wall shag carpeting, please refer to Chapter 11 and see Karma.

In any case, the choices you make for your home will say as much about you as the clothes you wear and the books you read. Here are a few themes to consider depending on the image you want to project:

The Ultra-Modern Minimalist Geometric shapes and angles are the key to a contemporary, modern motif. Metal, stone, glass, leather and solid colors are the elements, and artwork should be bold and large. Accessories are kept to a minimum, surfaces are kept clean and vertical blinds seal the deal.

What it says about you: You are cool, stylish and in control. You are independent and efficient with your money and your affections.

The Practical Contemporary Lighter, blonde woods are best for this modern, Scandinavian feeling. Woven fabrics or corduroys in brighter colors or cool blues and grays make for a calm, clean look. Retro furnishings can be mixed with more contemporary pieces, plants and eclectic artwork. The look is still modern, but more user-friendly than minimalism.

What it says about you: You are friendly and relaxed, neither fussy nor pretentious. You appreciate style, but it comes naturally and is unforced.

The Explorer/Adventurer Created by combining dark woods and textured fabrics for a warmer, heavier feeling. Indian, Latin or African art adds the sense of adventure, and exotic touches such as Moroccan rugs, paper lanterns and carved artifacts can be combined with framed photography and travel books for an international flair.

What it says about you: You are unpredictable and spontaneous, a thrill seeker who is also warm and sometimes sentimental, hard to pin down, but loyal and passionate.

The Sophisticated Gentleman Classic furniture and antiques are combined with stuffed bookshelves and warm, dark colors to create the feeling of an English library. Matching woods, leather armchairs, candles and heavy rugs make things cozy yet masculine at the same time. Frame some photos, some antique maps and throw a globe in the corner.

What it says about you: You are educated and knowledgeable. Confident and secure, you are a mentor, a teacher and a stable, trustworthy man of tradition.

The Rustic Bohemian Rough, weathered woods mixed with antiques, thrift-store finds and mismatched pieces can work together for an eclectic and comfortable space. Quirky doodads provide a touch of humor and wall space is filled with framed photos, postcards and various found oddities. Some consistency of color or recurring element is needed, however, to avoid total chaos and the appearance of insanity.

What it says about you: You are fun and easygoing, and you know what you like. You are a true individual with a sense of humor and easy charm.

An instant overhaul is not necessary to begin zeroing in on a particular style. You can get started by refinishing some of the pieces you have, then hit the flea market and pick up some key items. Replace furnishings one at a time. If you have your theme in mind, you can transform that dumpy den of yours faster than you think.

Smaller Spaces

Making the most of studio apartments and small spaces is not difficult. You can avoid the feeling of claustrophobia if you keep the furnishings to a minimum and section off areas with screens or by rearranging the furniture. Lighter color schemes and solid colors work best, and low ceilings can be combated by painting the ceiling a lighter color than the walls, and shining light toward the ceiling. Keeping your bed and seating low to the ground will also help to create an illusion of greater space.

Whatever look you're going for, it will be completely undermined if your place is too cluttered with junk for the style to be recognized. Removing anything that is useless will clear space and provide you with a cleaner canvas on which to work your magic.

Ten Great Space Savers

· Keep stacks of videos and CDs out of sight in an old chest or trunk.

· Replace oversized furniture with comfortable, smaller pieces.

· Store out-of-season clothes under the bed in plastic bins.

· Combine all electronic equipment in an armoire with closing doors.

· Replace bulky, extra chairs with small ottomans for additional, moveable seating.

· Install suspended lamps to clear surface space.

· Use a nonfunctioning fireplace to stack magazines or display plants.

· Hang shelves just below ceiling level for your book collection.

· Use area rugs to create a space within a space.

· Get rid of the roommate.

Walls

Once you know what you want to do with your furnishings, you can then turn to the finishing touches that will really define the space. Painting is, of course, the easiest way to liven up a room. Pale blues and greens as well as light neutrals can have a calming effect on jangled nerves, whereas brighter colors such as golds and reds can add energy and drama to a room.

When choosing a color at the paint store, always keep in mind that the color will look deeper and darker when it dries on the wall than it does on that small swatch you have in your hand. Also, if you choose to pair two colors together for contrast between walls and trim, get a second opinion to ensure that the colors really will work together.

Regardless of whether you decide to paint or not, there are a great many things you can do to make the most of those empty walls beyond hanging a cheesy seascape over the couch. And each wall can be treated in a different manner.

- Enlarge some personal photos from your travels, family photos of past generations or any other photographs of personal significance. Mat them and frame them in a variety of sizes and frames so that each one is unique, and fill a wall.
- Large mirrors, whether modern or antique, will add depth and dimension to a room. Smaller mirrors can also be combined in vertical or horizontal rows.
- Rather than buying a mass-produced print, try to find something unique like a painting by a street artist you come across on vacation, or something unusual from an antique shop or flea market.
- Create a combination of smaller mirrors, framed photos and other wall hangings and arrange them in an asymmetrical fashion to fill a wall.
- Hang rows of shelves, either short or long, vertically or horizontally on a wall for books or any other type of display.

Additional Touches

The smaller touches can make a big difference between a tasteful home and that of an overgrown man-child. The key is not to get carried away and stuff the place full of knickknacks like some sad, old spinster. Placing a few candles on a shelf or side table will add immeasurable ambience and make for a very seductive atmosphere in romantic situations. A few textured pillows tossed on the couch and the bed look great, and whatever tchotchkes you place on open surfaces should be tasteful and simple. These might include boxes, baskets, bowls, framed photos, coffee-table books or any other trinkets you've picked up in your travels.

Curtains and blinds are very important elements that are often overlooked. Just because the apartment came with mini-blinds doesn't mean you have no options. A curtain rod with simple fabric panels can be added on top of them or replace them altogether. In a more modern setting, blinds may be suitable, but they're magnets for dust so maintenance will be required. In general, however, curtains can be a great way to add color and style to your home. Prints can work well if the rest of the room isn't too cluttered, but fussy florals are probably not the way to go. When in doubt, opt for a good solid color or a simple print with clean lines. Stay away from complicated curtain systems with pulleys and pleats—just get some nice fabric panels and a straight rod.

Plants can also be used to add life and energy to a room, and you don't need a degree in botany to maintain them. If you're completely hopeless with other life-forms, you can always opt for a cactus or sturdy house plants such as aloes that require minimal care. Ferns should be avoided.

One of the easiest ways to spruce the place up, especially if you are "entertaining," is to place a few flowers in a vase. This is not to suggest that you want some ghastly bouquet that might have been lifted from a funeral parlor. A simple glass vase placed in the corner—it will look too self-conscious in the middle of the room—with solid-color tulips or other stem flower is perfectly sufficient. Don't worry, flowers aren't overly girly or pretentious, they just look really nice.

Lighting

A common mistake is underestimating the importance of lighting. There is no need to have your living room lit up like a soccer stadium, and there is plenty of wiggle room between floodlighting and complete darkness. You can begin by lowering the wattage of the light bulbs you're using. Softer lighting creates a relaxing mood, hides some of your cleaning oversights and is more flattering in general. If you really feel you need bright lights for certain situations, invest in dimmer switches to give you some control.

While most homes come with built-in lighting, they tend to be overhead lights that illuminate the entire room all at once. You can achieve far more appealing effects by choosing unique lamps, colored lampshades or lanterns and placing them at eye level for a lower light source. Combining soft lighting from lamps with carefully placed candles creates an impressive romantic setting, and allows you to regulate the lighting for the exact effect you want. Wall sconces are another excellent option as they bounce light off the walls, which always has a softening and stylish effect.

Wick Tip

Clip candle wicks to a quarter of an inch to avoid rapid burning and uneven melting of wax.

Aromatherapy

It is crucial to remember that a wide variety of unavoidable odors and smells will accumulate and intensify over time in your home. Food, smoke, animals, mold, body odor and unmentionable activities can all combine to create funky aromas that can take hold in your fabrics and furnishings. Just as you refresh your clothes by laundering them, you should refresh your home regularly with air fresheners, fabric-freshening sprays or even a simple antiseptic spray. It only takes a few seconds and it will keep your guests from wondering what on earth you've been up to when you're home alone.

Scented candles are an inexpensive and very effective way to control odors that may be lingering about the place. Earth-based fragrances such as sandalwood, sage, pine, citrus, cucumber and sea scents are light fragrances that aren't overly floral or reminiscent of granny's place. Bear in mind that you don't want to randomly mix and match scents just because you like the colors of the candles, or you may find your guests staggering about the place battling waves of nausea.

Tidiness vs. Cleanliness

Obviously, cleanliness is important if you're going to feel good about your home. If you can afford a maid, that's great, but if not, you're going to have to bite the bullet. You don't have to do it all at once, and you can do a room at a time if you choose. Occasional vacuuming and a spritz-and-wipe of all surfaces is good basic maintenance, but eventually you will have to do a little scrubbing in the kitchen and the bathroom.

That ring around your bathtub is not inevitable and permanent. Just grab a sponge and an abrasive cleaner the next time you step in the shower and get it over with. Likewise, giving the stovetop and countertops a quick once over is no big deal. But above all, you need to pay close attention to the bathroom sink and toilet. A grungy sink is bad enough, but nothing is nastier than a funky toilet, so don't let it get out of hand. Keep them both clean, and place a nice candle with a book of matches on the toilet tank.

Starting Points

Still not sure where to begin? You can start by eliminating the unforgivable and experimenting with a few simple fix-ups. As Confucius once said, "The journey of a thousand miles begins with the first step." So get walking.

Ten Things You Must Never Display in Your Home

- Posters
- Traffic signs
- Stuffed animals
- Neon beer signs
- Stackable storage crates
- Barcaloungers
- Cartoon bedsheets
- Random piles of videos or CDs
- Dirty dishes
- Anything to do with Barbra Streisand
- Underpants

**Never display
traffic signs...**

Ten Easy Fix-ups

- Paint white walls in warmer tones.
- Replace white lampshades with warmer colors.
- Define spaces within a room with area rugs.
- Mix and match cushions by color and texture on the couch and bed.
- Rearrange furniture in off-square angles.
- Fill the fireplace with candles.
- Enlarge, mat and frame personal photos.
- Refinish old dressers, tables or shelves.
- Place a simple glass vase with tulips or bamboo shoots in the corner.
- Fill a large bowl with lemons or apples as a coffee table centerpiece.
- Add some hard-to-kill plants or cacti to add life to the space.

**...or random piles of
videos or CDs**

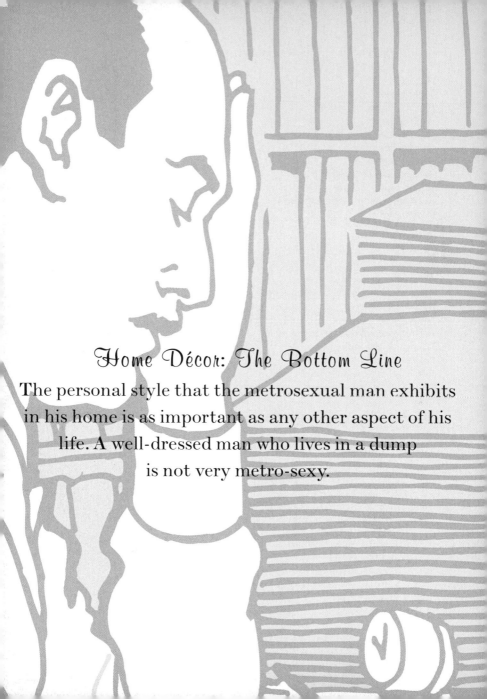

Home Décor: The Bottom Line

The personal style that the metrosexual man exhibits in his home is as important as any other aspect of his life. A well-dressed man who lives in a dump is not very metro-sexy.

No one can make you feel inferior...

...without your consent. —Eleanor Roosevelt

11

The Metrosexual Mind-set

The metrosexual male is optimistic about his
life, but not unrealistically so. He knows he has
choices and he actively seeks out the best options in any given situation.

The Power of Positivity

Imagine, if you will, a massive snowball at the top of a hill. At the base of the hill, there are two men standing side by side. The snowball begins to roll down the hill toward the two men, growing in size and speed. One of the men looks to the other and says, "Look at this. This kind of shit always happens to me. Look at it! It's headed right for me. Just watch. I'm telling you." The other man looks at the looming threat, looks back at the other man and then steps out of the snowball's path. The first man gets clobbered and his theory is proven correct. The second man goes skiing.

The moral of this simple story is that if you expect the worst to happen, it will. At all times, even in the most dire situations, you have a choice. You can focus on that which is wrong or that which is right. You can appreciate the beauty in people or you can look for their flaws. The assumptions you make about your own life often become true for you, and the assumptions you make about others can ruin relationships.

A negative mind-set goes way beyond your immediate perception of a given situation. Your attitude is perceptible to others. People notice if you are critical, cynical and angry at the world. It makes people pull away from you, it lessens your chances of promotion or advancement in the workplace, and it makes you a lousy date. And as you find yourself feeling rejected, overlooked and denied, you sink ever further into your black hole of isolation and resentment, and the situation worsens. This ridiculous cycle would be laughable if it weren't so destructive to so many lives.

Obviously life is never all sunshine and puppies, and nobody wants to be around a psychotically optimistic cheerleader, but a positive outlook and open mind have far more benefits than the obvious. Achieving a positive outlook is a matter of choice. Do not focus on the misery of being overweight—think about how good it will feel to be sexy, fit and strong. Do not wallow in the misery of your job—focus on your options and begin to visualize where you would like to be. The idea is to focus on what you want, and you will begin to move toward it. If you focus on the negative situation that is making you unhappy, you will stay there. Whether it's debt, loneliness or boredom, think about what you want to replace it with and hold onto that picture like a randy pitbull with a new chew toy.

Bear in mind, though, that there is no job, no lover and no financial status that will bring you happiness. True, these things may increase your enjoyment of life and relieve stress, but you cannot spend your life waiting to be rescued by any one of them. You should always have goals, but living your life with some distantly imagined finish line is a sad way to go. Your life is happening now. It may change in the future, but that doesn't mean that today doesn't count. Just because you are digging your way out of debt, that doesn't mean you can't go for a hike in the sunshine. Carrying a few extra pounds doesn't mean you can't find someone to love, and there are few situations in life that are truly inescapable.

One thing that is certain is that if you feel sorry for yourself, assume that you are powerless or decide that a situation is hopeless, there can only be one outcome. You will be sorry, powerless and hopeless. What you tell yourself on a daily basis slowly becomes true for you, so watch what messages you keep repeating to yourself. Any sports psychologist will tell you that if you constantly indulge in defeatist thinking, you will surely be defeated. You may have great challenges or obstacles in your path, but if you know what you truly want and are prepared to make it happen, there is nothing that you cannot achieve in one form or another. It all comes down to the little choices you make on a daily basis.

Always remember the basic facts:

- Your attitude is perceptible to others, and it determines how they react to you.
- Achieving a positive outlook is a matter of choice.
- Visualize what you want, and you will begin to move toward it.
- Obsess about the negative, and you will get more of the same.
- Don't look to others to rescue you from your unhappiness.
- Your moods and emotions are the result of your thoughts, and you can control your thoughts.
- Set goals for yourself, both short term and long term, both personal and professional.
- Outstanding debt doesn't preclude you from enjoying your life.
- View yourself as powerless, and you will be powerless.
- Your life is now.

Set goals for yourself, both short term and long term, both personal and professional.

Confidence

The metrosexual man is nothing if not confident, and the key to confidence is knowledge. It means knowing who you are, knowing your strengths and knowing your weaknesses. It is not a magical quality that some possess and others lack. It is an attainable state of mind that enables you to interact successfully with others, to achieve your goals and to move comfortably within a variety of social settings.

Confidence is not to be confused with arrogance. Whereas confidence is an inner sense of strength and calm, arrogance is an external display of bravado that is usually transparent. To be truly confident is to be truly comfortable with who you are. That's why the ugly rock star can become a sex symbol onstage. He's where he wants to be, he trusts that he belongs there and he is comfortable in his skin, despite any imperfections. That's sexy.

Confidence is also a matter of willpower and perseverance. You can't crawl into a hole and curl up into a ball every time things don't go your way. Confidence is earned by getting back on the horse and trying again, and by not personalizing every perceived rejection or defeat. If you don't get the job you applied for, it doesn't necessarily mean you weren't good enough. Maybe they hired the boss's daughter. Don't assume that because you got dumped you didn't measure up somehow. The other person may have issues you don't know about, or maybe it just wasn't meant to be. Just think it over, feel what you need to feel, then move onto the next thing. It's not always about you.

The Confident Metrosexual Always . . .

- Puts others at ease
- Takes responsibility for his actions
- Is aware of his sexuality
- Enjoys looking his best
- Flirts subtly
- Accepts flattery
- Is open to spontaneity
- Never loses control
- Tells the truth
- Is able to laugh at himself

Aware of his sexuality.

Lying, cheating and pretension undermine confidence. Behaviors such as these leave you at risk of being exposed, humiliated and rejected at any given time. They also burden you with the inescapable knowledge that you are weak and afraid. It may be argued that many people have gotten ahead in life through dishonest means, but on some level things always come undone, and a hefty price is paid. That's how they ended up on the evening news and that's why you found out what they did. It's called Karma.

Karma

Karma is a basic principle of the Hindu and Buddhist religions that is not so much a mystical belief as it is a logical premise based on the laws of cause and effect and human behavior. Though it does involve reincarnation and the atonement for crimes committed in past lives, it also applies very much to this lifetime and the here and now. At its core is the idea that the good and the bad that we experience in life has been earned. What goes around comes around. You get what you give. Or, as the Beatles sang, "And in the end, the love you take is equal to the love you make."

If you go through life being cruel and taking advantage of others, you will lose their trust and open yourself up to retaliation. If you are kind, friendly and outgoing, you will draw people of a similar nature into your orbit. If you are negative and bitter, you will subconsciously be seeking out others who are similarly disposed. It's not rocket science. Just bear in mind that if you allow yourself to be sucked into someone else's drama it means you are being manipulated.

It is always more effective to take the proverbial high road. You can respond honestly and calmly to confrontational situations, and still refuse to play the game. Just leave the offender standing there in his own little puddle of ugliness. Like the bully in the schoolyard, he will take it somewhere else, continue to make enemies and experience the typhoon of negativity that is his sad life. You, on the other hand, will have maintained your dignity and retained your power over what you will or will not allow in your life.

Humor

Mel Brooks once said, "Tragedy is when I cut my finger. Comedy is when you walk into an open sewer and die." Within this amusing observation lies a simple truth about the nature of humor—it is often derived at the expense of others. It is a lesson learned by most during childhood. While this premise still holds true in the adult world, hopefully the wisdom of age enables us to control our cruelty toward others.

The bottom line is that humor should always be light-hearted and inclusive. Don't isolate anyone, don't be insensitive and don't attempt to make yourself look better by putting someone else down. It will have the reverse effect. You are far better off expressing your wit through self-effacing humor, which, at its best, can be extremely charming and endearing. Laugh at yourself and . . . well, you know.

The Rules of Humor

Never laugh at
your own jokes.

- It is only acceptable to poke fun at that which a person can control.
- Making fun of anyone's physical limitations or characteristics is wrong.
- Social behavior, fashion, hairdos and sex provide much of life's great comedy, and are all fair game.
- The closer your relationship with friends and relatives, the greater leeway you have in your joking and banter.
- At its most effective, humor is seamlessly injected into the flow of conversation.
- Riddles are for children.
- Irony is always a big hit.
- If you want to be a stand-up comedian, get onstage.
- Subtlety of observation is the key to great wit.
- Never laugh at your own jokes.

The Open Mind

The further you advance in life, the greater the variety of people you will encounter. There is an infinite array of social scenes and lifestyles in this world and to be close-minded about any one of them is entirely self-defeating. Prejudice, bigotry or intolerance of others based on race, religion, sexual orientation, political affiliation or even fashion is small-minded and a sure sign of ignorance. Certainly, you aren't expected to like everyone you meet in life, but to disrespect or discount someone based on superficial assumptions is pointless.

Prejudice is a learned behavior. If you find yourself uncomfortable in the presence of any person or group of people, you need to ask yourself why that is. More often than not, it will be someone else's voice in your head that is making you uncomfortable. Get rid of that voice—it's holding you back. It's not unnatural to feel uncertain or self-conscious when encountering new situations or social customs, but how you deal with those feelings is entirely up to you. You can withdraw and stare at the aliens, or you can enjoy the curiosity and newness and respectfully deal with each person individually. Not every social setting will be your cup of tea, and that's fine. But if you find yourself tense and nervous when no real threat is present, a little self-examination is in order.

As in art, music and travel, an open mind will usually be rewarded with some unexpected surprises and new discoveries. The same holds true with people, so don't limit your social circles by rejecting anyone who is not immediately recognizable to you. This is not to suggest that you should rush forth and embrace the gang of hoodlums headed your way with bats and chains, but barring imminent danger, there is no reason to feel threatened or intimidated around anyone who is different from yourself. It may not be the drag queen who's making you feel uncomfortable, but rather your assumptions about what everyone else is thinking about you in relation to her. And if everyone else is having fun, why make yourself uncomfortable? And, truth be told, if there's a big old drag queen in the room, you're not the one being judged.

Action vs. Reaction
The actions you take determine the course of your life. Energy spent reacting to that which doesn't concern you is energy wasted.

Changing Your Life: Attitude and Resolve

At the end of the day, the metrosexual man understands that he is responsible for his own life. Regardless of his upbringing, his past or the obstacles in his path, it is up to him to make the changes that will improve the quality of his life. He can blame others and feel sorry for himself, or he can resolve to take charge and assert control over his life. It's his decision. That's your decision, too.

Even if you decide to do absolutely nothing and refuse to change, you are making a choice to stay where you are. On the other hand, you can choose the life you want to lead, and understand that the way you conduct yourself on a daily basis affects everything that happens to you. Attitude affects outcome, so check the negativity at the door.

Ten Things to Remember

- Believe that good things can happen to you.
- Find ways to slow down, relax and enjoy yourself.
- Make the effort to meet new people and try new things.
- Get enough sleep.
- Do whatever you can to improve yourself.
- Take a moment to compliment yourself when things go well.
- Take responsibility for your own shortcomings.
- Make an effort to nurture friendships and relationships.
- Pay attention to the little things.
- Do kind things for others without expecting a reward.

Do whatever you can to improve yourself.

Ten Things to Avoid

- Never let your inner voice put you down.
- Don't put yourself down in front of others.

- Try not to be suspicious of others without good reason.
- Don't judge others too quickly.
- Avoid indulging in self-pity.
- Never forget that there will always be greater and lesser people than yourself.
- Don't deny yourself pleasure and rewards.
- Never let fear stand in your way.
- Don't allow yourself to hide behind emotional walls.
- Don't be an asshole.

The Metrosexual Mindset: The Bottom Line
Your life is your own creation.
Make it a good one.

Michael Flocker

Michael Flocker has lived at various times amid the bright lights of Berlin, the fabulous chaos of New York and the hazy dream that is Los Angeles. His colorful career path has ushered him in and out of the worlds of fashion, film, television and travel writing. With this book he hopes to satisfy his lifelong urge to tell people how to live and behave. He currently lives in New York.

A note on the type

This book is set in 9-point Scotch Roman, an early 20th century revival design from the Monotype company. Scottish typefounders exerted a strong influence on the development of "transitional" typefaces, the bridge from "oldstyle" to "modern" designs. Scotch Roman typefaces were first cut by Englishman Richard Austin and cast by the Scottish typefounders Alexander Wilson & Son in Glasgow in the mid-18th century.

Captions, lists, and definitions are set in Benton Gothic, a typeface inspired by the "gothic" types of Morris Fuller Benton (1872-1948), including Franklin, Alternate, and News gothics. Benton was among the most prolific type designers of the 20th century, with over 180 designs to his credit.

The display type is Murray Hill, originally designed by Emil J. Klumpp for American Type Founders in 1956.

This book was designed and illustrated by George Restrepo and Alex Camlin. The pages were composed by Jane Raese and Christine Marra at Marrathon Productions. Printing by Edwards Brothers, Ann Arbor.